The Workforce Development Professional

Edward Kenny

Copyright © 2024 Edward Kenny

All rights reserved. No part of this book may be reproduced or transmitted in any form or by any means, electronic or mechanical, including photocopying, recording or by any information storage and retrieval system without permission in writing from the publisher.

Bluebird Publishing—Lindenhurst, New York
ISBN: 979-8-9859987-4-0
eBook ISBN: 979-8-9859987-5-7
Library of Congress Control Number: 2024916751
Title: *The Workforce Development Professional*
Author: Edward Kenny
Digital distribution | 2024
Paperback | 2024

Dedication

This book is dedicated to the memory of Melinda Mulawka Mack.

Disclaimer

Neither the publisher nor the author is engaged in rendering professional advice or services to the reader. The ideas, suggestions, and procedures provided in this book are not intended as a substitute for seeking professional guidance. The author is not an attorney or an accountant and does not represent or speak on behalf of the federal, state, or any other government agency or other organization. Nothing in this book should be interpreted as a definitive legal, regulatory or policy interpretations, advice or opinions. Neither the publisher nor the author shall be held liable or responsible for any loss or damage allegedly arising from any suggestion or information contained in this book. Always seek direction, and/or advice from the appropriate governing authorities that oversee your operations. Access the services of attorneys and/or accountants, as required.

Table of Contents

Introduction..ix
Chapter I: Professionalism...1
Chapter II: Passion...5
Chapter III: Enthusiasm...8
Chapter IV: The System 10
Chapter V: Serving Special Populations through
 Systems within Systems......................................32
Chapter VI: The System, Center, Program Paradox............35
Chapter VII: Achieving Customer Satisfaction
 with Products That Melt 43
Chapter VIII: Career Services..................................46
Chapter IX: Performance Leadership 60
Chapter X: Return-on-Investment 73
Chapter XI: Moving Beyond Business Services,
 or Are Your Business Services B.S.?.................79
Chapter XII: Work-Based Training 102
Chapter XIII: Youth..112
Chapter XIV: The Great White Whale and Other Grants...124
Chapter XV: If This Is an Emergency… 130
Chapter XVI: Fiscal 134
Chapter XVII: Having "The Talk" with Kids.....140
Acknowledgements...141
Final Note 143
Bibliography 145
About the Author 148

Introduction

The Workforce Development Professional offers help to readers who may be in pursuit of their best selves, both personally and professionally. Workforce development professionals can be found in just about every sector of employment such as:

- government
- education
- economic development
- community-based organizations
- corporations
- libraries and many other fields.

This industry offers unique challenges and opportunities to the people who toil in its fields every day. The nature of our work at times seems paradoxical. For example, our resources and operations usually increase in a poor economy. The opposite occurs when unemployment rates are low. When the great majority of the available workforce is employed, organizations tend to minimize the importance or need for workforce development professionals to function. However, workforce development remains crucial. If companies strive to empower the workforce development system when the economy and labor market is favorable, we might better prevent high unemployment rates in the future. We succeed when the system has the resources it needs to establish and maintain the pipeline of skilled workers that businesses require to prosper under any economic condition.

Another paradox that can often impact a workforce development professional is the existence of expenditure mandates, which sometimes require that funds be spent in short periods of time, while at other junctures we may find it difficult to meet our expenses and adequately address the demands of our customers, both job seekers and businesses. Ours is primarily a publicly-funded system empowered by legislation over many years. And yet, the system and the jobs of the people who maintain it, are often misunderstood.

We must maintain legal compliance and fully comprehend the laws that fund us, while at the same time employing maximum flexibility and creativity. In this regard, a true workforce development professional will use both sides of their brain and will avoid lamenting, *"I am not a numbers person,"* or *"I cannot get bogged down in the law,"* or objections like, *"I can only deal with data, statistics, or the bottom line."* Workforce development jobs should be considered a science and an art. It is a peculiar mix that makes these roles not only interesting, but a source of gratification. With this understanding, it is important that readers of this book, regardless of which side of the brain they tend to favor, do not blast past the dense, sometimes lengthy legal quotations that are presented. This is because the technical information provided is the springboard for our creative vision.

Launching from that springboard, the challenges faced by aspiring workforce development professionals may represent opportunities to create, innovate, build, and serve. This transformation of challenges into opportunities is historically evident in our ability to maximize meager resources through creative service protocols to target the most in need at times when the system is overwhelmed by demand.

Conversely, we have historically helped people advance through career pathways, during times when unemployment rates are low and entry level jobs are in great supply. Workforce development professionals exhibit the business acumen necessary to leverage resources from new and previously untapped sources. And our systems have become more recognizable and ubiquitous through fundamentally sound marketing and advocacy techniques.

The Workforce Development Professional describes how the existential challenges of our industry can be met and how opportunities might be seized through the individual and group dynamics of professionals, who by-and-large, are hard-working, dedicated, well-informed, passionate, enthusiastic and imaginative. History has taught us that the Workforce Innovation and Opportunity Act of 2014 will one day be repealed and replaced by new legislation, thus leading to new requirements, methods, techniques, priorities, and philosophies that will ultimately affect our work. Of course, this means that portions of this book will, over time, become obsolete. In fact, a sequence of local and global events yet to come, along with other factors such as societal evolution, cultural changes, and technological advancements, will reshape the world as we perceive it, even as you are reading this now. Nevertheless, certain values and philosophies are as timeless and relevant to any place in time, as is the enduring spirit of humanity.

With this in mind, hopefully these pages will be useful in your pursuit of unlocking and fully realizing your own potential, and will be of assistance to you in your goal of prospering within the honorable and essential field you have chosen not only as an occupation, but also as a life passion. Best of luck on your journey to and throughout the space of workforce development professionalism.

Chapter I
Professionalism

What do you do for a living? At some point, all of us will have to field this question. It could be at a barbecue, a family gathering, at a gym, on a date, or just about anywhere. When I first entered the workforce development trade, I struggled to offer a response that the questioner would find relatable. My struggle pertained both to the description of what we now call "workforce development" and to the word "professional." At that time, occupations in the field of workforce development seemed below the status of "professional."

I entered the field in the late 1970's when the *Manpower Development and Training Act* (MDTA) program was replaced by the *Comprehensive Employment and Training Act* (CETA) program. In those days, the lack of a brand and image for our field resulted in workplace development being referred to as *unemployment, welfare,* or *CETA*, the latter often morphing into "cedar" like the tree, through mispronunciation. Using those limited terms to describe where we worked and what we do, it came as no surprise that public perception of our occupation was often limited and devaluing. In those days, a doctor was a professional, a lawyer was a professional, and a certified public accountant was a professional. My goal at the time, when I was asked how I earned a living, was not to boast or cower, but to answer the question truthfully while preserving my dignity. Unfortunately, when I explained that I was a job developer, along with providing the name of the organization I worked for, the evaluation that followed was that I was one wrung on the career ladder above unemployment myself, receiving public assistance, and/or being covered with sap from a cedar tree.

While there should be no shame attached to these conditions, well except maybe for the sap part, suffice it to say that with the impression of our field being either negative or non-existent, workforce development professionals had bigger problems than impressing people at parties.

Lack of appreciation for what we do, misunderstanding of who we are, and an overall lack of awareness for this industry individually or collectively, represented fatal blows to the workplace development profession in terms of our growth, success, and of course, our funding. Those blows not only undermined us as people, but could even have harmed or destroyed workforce development as a profession, leading to a disruption or termination of the essential services we provide to job seekers, their families, communities, and to the economic well-being of our country.

Although many intrepid professionals in our field continued their good work, undaunted by the heavy yoke of this inaccurate, or sometimes, non-existent image, a breakthrough change was needed. For me and many other similarly situated workers in this arena, that breakthrough change was initiated and accelerated in the late 1980s by the creation of the New York Association of Training and Employment Professionals, Inc. (NYATEP).

The leaders who founded NYATEP were from local areas in the state of New York. John Twomey, its first Executive Director, gave structure and depth to occupations in workforce development that elevated them from jobs to professions. NYATEP created collegial forums through which local workforce professionals could commiserate with each other. Twomey also created a firm space for them to interact with their funding organizations and regulators. We gained strength through collaboration, not only with each other, but with the state and federal government.

One of those collaborations was established between NYATEP and the New York State Department of Labor, resulting in the convening of the majority of the local workforce development board staff leadership with the Labor Department leadership on a regular basis as a collegial working group.

Through NYATEP, we not only learned how the "sausages" of legislation, grants, programs and even audits were made, but we also gained the capacity, without violating lobbying laws, to impact those processes for the better. As members of NYATEP, we earned the opportunity to put our actions where our mouths were. This affected policy in state and federal meetings. It also allowed us to gain recognition for excellence, share promising practices, develop strategies to gain allies, and combat those who were something other than allies, all while continually creating and enriching traditional and non-traditional partnerships.

NYATEP supported us with a reservoir of expertise that included the talent of its board of directors and their staff, NYATEP's staff, its lobbyists, and expert consultants. It also partnered with other state workforce associations to apply a "strength in numbers" approach to affecting change. In my opinion, NYATEP evolved in the image of John Twomey insomuch as it was visionary, always ahead of the curve, dedicated to making the workforce development system the best it could and should be for the sake of all of its constituencies. It challenged its members to keep up with the pace of progress, articulating the empirical raison d'être, all the while, maintaining a spirit of compassion and a sense of humor.

Through the years, NYATEP and its members have stayed true to that image, continuing under the able leadership of Melinda Mack and beyond to reflect an image of the people who work in the field of workforce development as "professionals."

It would help any aspiring workforce development professional to collaborate and also become a part of NYATEP.

There are also other progressive and helpful state and national workforce development associations that have been pioneers that have contributed to the growth and success of our industry and the professionals that these organizations represent. Two of the national organizations to be counted in this number are the National Association of Workforce Boards (NAWB) and the National Association of Workforce Development Professionals (NAWDP). The latter organization administers the Certified Workforce Development Professional certification program. In addition, the United States Department of Labor Employment and Training Administration operates a helpful capacity-building resource entitled, "Workforce GPS," which is described on its web site as follows:

"WorkforceGPS is sponsored by the Employment and Training Administration (ETA) of the U.S. Department of Labor to connect workforce professionals, educators, and business leaders to useful technical assistance resources. Here you will find curated communities of interest, webinars, training resources, and data-driven strategies to help develop efficient and effective approaches for results-driven employment programs. By fostering collaboration

and providing evidence-based insights, WorkforceGPS advances ETA's goal of building a skilled workforce that drives economic opportunity and business prosperity..."[1]

---

[1] https://www.workforcegps.org

Chapter II
Passion

Passion. No, this is not a romance novel, unless falling in love with the workforce development industry qualifies as romance. That's what happened to me, due in no small part to what I learned at an early stage in my career, which is the importance of passion. I was twenty-three years old when I started working for a federally-funded county employment and training program. Despite being hired about a year and half after graduating from college and lacking experience in the field, fortunately, I knew that many of my superiors and co-workers saw potential in me. My question, however, was *potential for what?* As workforce development professionals, we should never forget that most college graduates enter the workplace with very little understanding of what potential refers to. Throughout my career, I observed this phenomenon and was able to empathize through my own experiences.

Perceiving that the "ship" of my career was demonstratively seaworthy, while my "compass" was weak, some kindhearted staff directed me to the resident office guru. We will call him Dr. Tipps. Circa 1977, I worked in an office comprised of approximately 150 people that operated the CETA Program. At that point in the evolution of federal workforce legislation, a "prime sponsor," i.e., the program operator, could afford to include a resident "brain" among its planning staff. The planning department was so large and complex, it was necessary for me to make an appointment to speak with this roving Ph.D. Our exchange was brief, as we conversed in a doorway. To this day, I still appreciate his sincere attempt to listen to my complaints about not knowing what to do with my life and his willingness to offer a solution.

First, Dr. Tipps asked what did I major in, when I was in college? To which I replied, "Business Management." He then said, "It seems to me that someone who majored in business management should be running a business." After his words echoed through my somewhat empty young head, I responded candidly, "I am not interested in running a business." The comical irony of my response was not lost on me, as I am sure it was not lost on him. Yet, the guru forged ahead and without passing judgment said, "Whatever you do, you need to develop a passion for your work."

Although his advice may have sounded trite on the surface, his words had a profound effect on how I approached my work. Of course, change did not happen overnight. I returned to my regular job duties, which at the time were those of a job developer, where I was essentially tasked with selling jobs to people and selling people to jobs. And yet, something was different. I began to read on my own, researching interviewing techniques. I learned as much as I could about the job seekers that I interviewed, and about the employers I attempted to refer them to, or placed them with. Without overstating the importance of the advice to be passionate about my work, it is safe to say that those few minutes with a caring adviser changed the approach I had taken with my career, and ultimately my life. An argument could be made that the advice was only a tuft that coincidentally hit my sail just as I was drawing my own gust from achieving a state of inner awareness, readiness and maturity. My response is that it does not matter from which direction or what source the wind came. What matters is that I was moved and my adviser played a part in that movement.

Herein lies a lesson I feel all workforce professionals could benefit from... even during the briefest exchange between a career counselor and a job seeker, a life can be significantly changed for the better in an instant. This advice also lends itself to marketing staff, employers, management, elected officials, public relations staff, workforce development board members, and their staff, and even the media. The power of these interactions exists in all walks of life, including, teachers, coaches, clergy, supervisors, nurses, and parents.

We may not perceive the effect we have on children and adults at the time of the interaction, but looking back, particularly from the perspectives of those we have interacted with, we can appreciate how a person's life journey was either helped, hindered, or an opportunity to help was sadly missed. Or in the worst-case scenario, the "professional" had a negative, rather than a positive impact on the job seeker. While acknowledging my own imperfections and failures in general, I have always tried to maintain an awareness of the responsibility with which I have been entrusted as a parent, a coach and as a workforce development professional.

In terms of the latter, I recommend that we always maintain our focus, empathy and that we look for synergistic opportunities. We should approach every interaction with job seekers and the other constituencies mentioned above as if we are entering their lives for a higher purpose beyond our understanding. It is my hope that we apply all of our intelligence, skills, and talents to fulfill that purpose and responsibility in a positive way.

The predicate for this application is our passion. It is something that will be sensed by all of those we see to help, whose help we seek, those we wish to partner with, those we seek to follow, and those we seek to lead. Passion leads to enthusiasm.

Chapter III
Enthusiasm

Workforce development professionals should approach their jobs as experts in the field, thus acting more in a consultative capacity than as a bureaucrat encumbered by routine and procedure. Furthermore, if you find a way to love what you do, then you will be enthused and your enthusiasm will become contagious.

Without offending the perpetually perky portion of the population, I wish to clarify that one can be enthusiastic without having a bubbly personality. For example, when a Cy Young Award-winning major league pitcher toes the rubber and stares in at the batter, his continence is almost like that of a mythic sheriff of the Wild West in the nineteenth century. Is he enthused? You bet, but he controls his emotions and times out the perfect application of his pitching motion, marshaling intellect, power, precession and grace in proper balance. Clearly, he loves his job and is a master at it, but his enthusiasm is channeled into a process that achieves *Hall of Fame* type outcomes.

The jobs of career counselors and those of many others in the field of workforce development are equally as important as a professional baseball player, at any level, provided that they are performed by enthusiastic professionals. The role of employment and training offices in America evolved from agencies who serve "trapped" customers to service centers for "demanding" customers. In the 1990s the United States Department of Labor introduced the "Enterprise," an organization of the highest quality workforce development organizations in the Nation. Founded on the Malcolm Baldrige Performance Excellence Program[2], I feel that the Enterprise fostered a sense of enthusiasm and pride of workmanship among

---

[2] https://www.nist.gov

workforce development leaders throughout the United States. Because quality management requires a state of continuous improvement, workforce development leaders understood that the type of "enthused professional" embodied by the pitcher in the example above, must be characterized by more than good intentions. Such an individual must be the expert, or at least passionately desire to evolve into the expert that their customers deserve and expect. Of course, the workforce professional you encounter should be friendly, kind, empathetic and compassionate, but that professional should also be an individual at the top of their game who will support and guide you to achieve your career goals. In short, enthusiasm should begin, but not end, with a friendly greeting, and ultimately, should achieve professional results.

Chapter IV
The System

Imagination is a gift that the workforce development professional should appreciate, cultivate and apply. Like many such gifts, because I believe that human beings are endowed with a free will, imagination may be used for the greater good, or for opposite purposes. A person who truly aspires to become a workforce development professional, should seek to use the gift of imagination in the most positive sense. It should manifest as a quiet and internal sense of awareness that you are doing the right things, at the right times, in an honorable field of endeavor.

Although the point of this achievement is not simply to gain public recognition, you will feel a sense of well-deserved respect for your persistence, hard work, and integrity. At the same time, just like an everyday major league baseball player, you will occasionally make errors, go into slumps, and lose. While you will not become immune to falling, you can still develop the ability to rise when you fall. To do so, you must maintain your passion, your enthusiasm and always do your very best, every day. If you fail to persist in this way, the vaunted title of workforce development professional, once attained with honor and determination, may be diminished or disappear. The level of persistence required of a workforce development professional is in direct proportion to the scope of that individual's imagination. This is because imagination is the primary point of conception for our workforce development systems.

Over the years there have been many iterations of federal workforce development legislation. After entering the field just after the Manpower Development and Training Act (MDTA) Program ended, I worked for programs funded by the Comprehensive Employment and Training Act (CETA), then the Job Training Partnership Act (JTPA), the JTPA Amendments, the Workforce Investment Act (WIA) and the Workforce Innovation and Opportunity Act (WIOA).

In my opinion, regardless of what legislation is in place, a workforce development professional must be well-acquainted with the federal statutes, federal regulations (i.e., Code of Federal Regulations, Final Rule) promulgated by the United States Department of Labor; Training and Employment Guidance Letters issued by the United States Department of Labor, state laws, and policies. Also, the preamble to federal regulations can provide insight into the intention of the framers.

Federal funding for "the system" that is required to be established under WIOA is appropriated by the U.S. Congress and then allocated via a funding formula to each individual state, and subsequently allocated by formula to local workforce development areas within the state. Allocations within the states are based upon state designated local workforce development areas. Once a local area is designated, the chief elected official of that area is required to appoint a local workforce development board. The local chief elected official, who is the local grant recipient under WIOA, may establish a local grant sub-recipient and fiscal agent to administer the WIOA adult, youth and dislocated worker programs. The local workforce development board is required to select a one-stop operator through a competitive procurement process.

One might argue that the laws, regulations and policies described above are the conception point of the workforce development system, but in my view, the system does to come alive until workforce development professionals read, absorb and meditate on those documents, and then, imagine how they might be implemented. From that perspective, the laws, regulations and policies, which might be abbreviated as "the rules," are not necessarily constraints or even boundaries, but rather the foundation of an endeavor for the greater good that is bound only by our imaginations.

If your reaction to these thoughts on "imagination" is that you play too small of a role in the workforce development system to make a difference, let us employ the analogy of an airline company worker. Without baggage handlers, airplane cleaners and ticket agents, the aircraft essentially cannot fly. A pilot must wait for people in these professions to complete their tasks before taking off. At the same time, a pilot is subservient to the air traffic controllers and on and on. If you are a cleaner now, it is conceivable that you might one day own the airline company. More far-fetched dreams have been realized.

My career, like those of many of my colleagues, took me from a long line of menial jobs during grammar school, high school and college before I entered the workforce development industry. As previously stated, my first assignment of many in the workforce field was as a job developer. That ultimately led to several leadership positions. This included serving on the board of directors of NYATEP, serving on local advisory councils for education, economic development and workforce development, in addition to serving on the staff of a local workforce development board. Although those positions were not always in a chief executive capacity, there were many opportunities to use my imagination, to conceive of a vision, and then to implement and realize that vision.

So where is the connection between imagination and the workforce development system? The answer is "everywhere." As mentioned in the *Introduction*, workforce development professionals at all levels should use both sides of their brain to be creative and imaginative, caring and compassionate, emotionally enthusiastic and passionate on one side, while using the other side to be logical, accountable, legally compliant and scientific. The system should be constructed in this same human image, meaning it has a brain and a heart.

There are those individuals who might argue that imagination is suffocated in a highly regulated environment. I challenge these individuals to understand that their rejection of the coexistence of the brain and the heart of a workforce development system is naïve, short-sighted, and possibly the product of cynicism, selfishness and laziness. In the field of workforce development, when a person laments that they are unable to be a visionary, creative, or compassionate because of regulatory restrictions, they are either intentionally or unintentionally missing the whole point of why their job exists. This is especially true of those in leadership positions.

I am not trying to ignore the negative impact, or even the strangling effect of over-regulation. In fact, I agreed with those who, during the Enterprise initiative, sought to identify and eliminate "stupid rules." The irony is that, among those who were combating the stupid rules were government bureaucrats above the local level, including state and federal officers. From their perspective, many of the stupid rules were not imposed in response to regulatory requirements, which was a claim sometimes falsely made, but rather invented on a local level.

The beauty of the Enterprise movement was that it created collegial forums on equal footing for federal, state, local, public and private stakeholders to collaborate in the interest of continuous improvement. And continuous improvement is not just an impressive sounding and widely acceptable catch phrase that we should speed past without contemplation. Why should we aspire to continually improve? One reason, which is perhaps the generally approved rationale, is that it has become inculcated into the highest evolution of organizational management culture.

Another reason is that it is the moral imperative of human beings working in a service capacity, including those who populate the organizations that perform workforce development system functions, to do what is right for their customers. While both of these rationales are sound, there exists yet another reason. Failure to improve and/or to have systems in place for continuous improvement, particularly when the establishment and operation of such systems has become a staple of modern management culture, would leave workforce development systems, and the organizations who comprise them, as well as their staff, vulnerable to consequences ranging from criticism to extinction. Therefore, continuous improvement to the workforce development system is about competition, morality and survival. Nevertheless, there are some, often the same folks who lament the constriction of the regulations under government programs, who are the ones who impose their own restrictions, who fail to embrace modern practices of continuous improvement, as well as other progressive initiatives.

As a qualifying statement, I stipulate that not all new, progressive or different practices are effective. Sometimes it "ain't broke" and therefore should not be fixed. However, ironically, opposition to regulations or promising practices is sometimes offered by individuals who actually have not read or comprehended them. My point is not to criticize those individuals, many of whom might be highly accomplished in other ways and motivated by laudable callings. My point is to turn the gaze of the aspiring professional toward what might be an unseen horizon, beyond the view of those who might discourage them. After dispatching the naysayers, we must embark upon a journey that leads to the coveted vista of the best workforce development system that we can imagine.

Before we begin our journey, we must be supplied with the provisions we will need to reach our destination. Those provisions include knowledge, an adventurous spirit, optimism, belief in ourselves, a strong work ethic, integrity, determination and discipline. The provision of knowledge includes an intimate familiarity with workforce development legislation and regulations. Earlier, I stated that "the laws, regulations, and policies, which might be abbreviated as 'the rules,' are not necessarily constraints or even boundaries, but rather the foundation of an endeavor for the greater good that is only bound by our imaginations." Being well-versed in the "rules" is, as stated earlier, the foundation upon which our creative ideas can be constructed. This is not to disagree that a danger lurks in getting caught in a maze of red tape, but also, as stated earlier, the true workforce development professional can use both sides of the brain to maximum capacity.

With this in mind, local boards should lay the foundation for imagining a local workforce development system by understanding the rules. With that understanding we may build upward to the pinnacle of our creativity. The first component of the local workforce development system addressed by the WIOA statute is the establishment of local workforce development boards, which is described under WIOA Section 107. That description includes the requirement for state governors to appoint and certify local boards, as well as the requirements for local membership appointment, certification and recertification processes.

Section 107(3) states:

"The members of the local board shall elect a chairperson for the local board from among the representatives described in paragraph (2)(A)."[3]

The above passage requires that the board include at least one officer and that the officer must be selected from the business members of the board through an election process. Most boards, at their own discretion and in accordance with their own bylaws, either elect or appoint additional officers, such as a vice chairperson. This simple, brief and somewhat inexorable requirement bears significant

---

[3] Public Law 113-128, Section 107(b)(3)

gravity for the workforce development professional who is working to construct a system. The profundity of this passage, in my view, is that the board, as part of the governance structure of the local system, must have its own governance structure.

The local workforce development boards under WIOA and under its predecessor, WIA, possess greater power of governance than their counterparts under previous legislation, such as private industry councils established under JTPA. To be a workforce professional is to accept and accommodate changes that new legislation requires. Once the legislation becomes law and the final regulations are promulgated, the workforce professional must dutifully establish and maintain a workforce development system that complies with the letter and the spirit of those rules.

I caution those who might feel the urge to bend, avoid, or even break rules to reconsider their intentions. The penalties are too severe for non-compliance and the rewards are too great to realize success while maintaining your integrity. Sadly, in any endeavor, including workforce development, those who stray from the guidance of their moral compass, often do so slowly, almost imperceptibly, only to be shocked to realize how far they have wandered from who they once thought they were and who they aspired to be. A metaphor for this phenomenon is a sleeping sailor in small row boat that is tethered to a dock. In the dark of the night, without the sailor noticing, the little boat becomes untethered in an instant and begins to float away, slowly, but inexorably from the shoreline. When the sailor awakens, feeling only a few seconds have passed, the boat is far out to sea and away from the shoreline. Do not let your character "slip away" and refrain from small indiscretions, deceptions, exceptions, and other misdeeds. They will always come back to haunt you and you are better than that.

Those leaders who cannot rise to the challenge of new legislation or the evolution of existing legislation will inevitably wander, perhaps ever so slightly, sometimes almost imperceptibly, away from the spirit and the letter of the workforce legislation into a non-compliant and dysfunctional status. Their plight could be compared to an aviator that is slightly off course and who, without proper flying adjustments, at first moves only centimeters away in the wrong direction, but in the fullness of time, flies thousands of miles away from the desired destination. The workforce professional must not waste time in lamenting the rules, or arguing about their inability to immediately change them, or denying that they exist, or in ignoring them. Instead, we must find creative ways to fulfill the rules while creating and implementing not only a system that is productive, but ideally, one that attains a world class designation. Even the most progressive and diligent workforce development professional will be repeatedly challenged to manage the process of change and once again need to imagine anew.

From my perspective, the WIOA framers seem to nudge us to be imaginative in the process of system-building by encouraging the establishment of "standing committees" in Section 107(b) (4) (A) (i) (iii) (B), which states:

"(A) IN GENERAL.—The local board may designate and direct the activities of standing committees to provide information and to assist the local board in carrying out activities under this section. Such standing committees shall be chaired by a member of the local board, may include other members of the local board, and shall include other individuals appointed by the local board who are not members of the local board and who the local board determines have appropriate experience and expertise. At a minimum, the local board may designate each of the following:

(i) A standing committee to provide information and assist with operational and other issues relating to the one-stop delivery system, which may include as members representatives of the one-stop partners.

(ii) A standing committee to provide information and to assist with planning, operational, and other issues relating to the provision of services to youth, which shall include community-based organizations with a demonstrated record of success in serving eligible youth.

(iii) A standing committee to provide information and to assist with operational and other issues relating to the provision of services to individuals with disabilities, including issues relating to compliance with section 188, if applicable, and applicable provisions of the Americans with Disabilities Act of 1990 (42 U.S.C. 12101 et seq.) regarding providing programmatic and physical access to the services, programs, and activities of the one-stop delivery system, as well as appropriate training for staff on

providing supports for or accommodations to, and finding employment opportunities for, individuals with disabilities.

(B) ADDITIONAL COMMITTEES.—The local board may designate standing committees in addition to the standing committees specified in subparagraph (A)."[4]

The above passage allows a committee structure which can help to create a more effective board. Local leaders may not embrace the committee structure, because of the fear of rogue committees, which they might believe will lead to a rogue board. This fear might arise, in part, due to the lack of sufficient staffing of the board. One element of that limitation might be the amount of funds allocated to board staff. In the case of an incorporated board, there is likely a budget item that establishes this limitation. In the case of an unincorporated board, while funding is a consideration, the local government, or a designated unit of local government must decide how many and what type of staff to deploy. How this decision is made and who makes it can be a predictor of success or failure. Will this decision about how the board is staffed be made by leaders who are passionate, enthusiastic and imaginative in their perception of the workforce development system? Or by those with opposite characteristics? Or perhaps, by those whose outlook lies somewhere in between? They cannot reach this understanding without intellectually absorbing the legislation.

With a properly deployed contingent of board staff, even if that contingent is only one person, I believe that the committee structure is, in the long run, not only cost efficient, but one which will usually help create and maintain an efficient system that yields excellent results. I also believe that a workforce development system should not be limited to conducting day-to-day "retail" services for job seekers and businesses. This means that staff must perform tasks beyond the realm of interviewing and referring job seekers to jobs, enrolling job seekers into training programs, writing job orders, and the like. My vision of a modern, high-functioning workforce development system calls for staff to perform important and different functions that require a board staff. Those functions are the glue that holds the structure of the board and its committees together,

---

[4] Public Law 113-128, Section 107(b)(4)(A)(i)(iii)(B)

and the board and its committees are critical portions of the brain and the heart of the system. Because the board is the organizational leadership and oversight infrastructure that makes the system possible, workforce development professionals who embrace these concepts would be unfulfilled serving a board that is not ambitious.

Conversely, they will be professionally stimulated serving on boards that are engaged, well-attended, helpful, supportive and resourceful. Board business that is vetted through committees is more credible. Board members who serve on committees become better informed and often will advocate for the work that we do. The partners and the connections that these members maintain will enrich the depth and breadth of the board, with the ultimate impact of developing more jobs, higher wages, more retention and a higher skilled workforce. Boards that possess vibrant standing committees, and indeed, impactful ad hoc committees or work groups, as required, will be able to conduct more energetic and productive full membership meetings. And the quality of board meetings is of paramount importance. Without quality meetings, the board and its committees will lose the best members, those who can spot lack of commitment to excellence, and those who are passionate about service, but who might become disillusioned if board members seem disinterested.

I once heard a story about a member of a board, who when asked what he thought about his local board meeting responded "I think we need to have a meeting about how to have a meeting." To some that might sound like a call to create the bureau of bureaucracy, in other words, he might sound like someone extensively married to procedure. On the contrary, I would argue that just as you have a better baseball game if you go over the ground rules before the game, so too, by establishing guidelines for the conduct of a meeting, a professional tone is established. This tone is important because we cannot achieve the status of a workforce development professional without always conducting ourselves and our business in a professional manner. That includes drafting a clear and an inexorably logical agenda, not overwhelming members with references or handouts, but providing enough background information and reading material, to clarify the discussion. In cases where motions are required to adopt actions, the members should understand what will be requested at the onset of any related presentations or discussions. The relevance of agenda items and board business will only be reinforced when it emanates from the pre-work of standing committees.

The following are examples of some committees that might be useful to the workforce development board:

- Executive Committee
- Youth
- Partner Organizations
- Special Populations
- Business Services
- Quality
- Grant Strategic Planning Team and/or Steering Committees.

You may or may not wish to include some of the examples in the list, or you might wish to include them in addition to others. Established and maintained properly, they do serve important purposes. For example, an executive committee provides a leadership structure for the full membership. An effective executive committee should, at the very least, include the chairperson, as well as a vice chairperson, who could lead meetings in the absence of the chair. Since the requirement under WIOA law is that standing committees are chaired by board members, in the interest of maintaining a well-informed and relevant executive committee, it makes sense to add standing committee chairpersons to the executive committee. The development of agenda items and the planning of meetings to ensure quality are within the sweet spot of the executive committee.

I can hear the arguments from some who would demur those volunteers, especially people from the business sector, cannot devote the time that this committee work requires. My response is:

(A) Do you know that for a fact? Have you tried to make your passion, enthusiasm, imagination and professionalism contagious? This is important work we are doing because it affects our businesses, our workers, our economy, our quality of life and our economy.

(B) As a workforce professional your job will seldom be easy. Hopefully, you are in your position because you have demonstrated the talents and qualifications necessary to get things done, with one of those talents including a knack for motivation and deployment of volunteers to dedicate themselves to working for a good cause.

All workforce development board meetings and standing committee meetings should be attended by the workforce development board director or designated board staff. Minutes of all meetings of each of these bodies must be shared with the full membership and posted on the local workforce development system web site. Not only do these postings ensure technical compliance with sunshine laws, but they establish a culture of transparency which a variety of constituencies will appreciate. In addition, posted minutes create a legacy of documentation that will help bring new members, partners and staff up to speed, while serving as a reference for those who have been actively participating in the system.

There is also a strong case to be made for creating a youth standing committee because youth issues are quite different, in many respects, from those of adults and dislocated workers. Partner organizations should meet and interact regularly, whether or not they are identified as a standing committee. WIOA creates a great opportunity for partner collaboration, blending and braiding of funds, which foster integration and efficiency. The streamlining and focused application of partner programs in a workforce development system is one of the greatest opportunities for imaginative planning that a workforce professional will encounter. Special populations standing committees can marshal the resources of new partners to create systems within the system that break new ground in serving a host of special populations, such as individuals with disabilities, offenders, veterans, older workers, and any other groups that you might wish to focus on.

A standing committee for business services creates an ideal opportunity to recruit businesses to market to their peers. An essential component of world class businesses services is moving beyond job development functions to establish meaningful and mutually beneficial <u>relationships</u> with business partners. Not only does a standing committee provide a forum for fostering these partnerships, it often results in support from business members in terms of marketing resources, provision of meeting space, advocacy, even financial support, and all of the prestige that goes with those contributions.

The establishment of a standing committee for quality moves discussions and planning sessions beyond the dull reporting and analysis of seemingly opaque statistics, into engaging strategic sessions, which can be cross-referenced with other committee work, such as marketing and special populations. It would not only be awkward, but also, unethical for board staff alone to essentially tell the board if its plans are working well or not. By engaging board members, and possibly other committee members in quality strategic planning, the board takes greater ownership in its own activities and the outcomes of those activities.

Based on my experience in conceiving of governance and planning structures for specific grant projects, I recommend establishing Grant Strategic Planning Teams and/or Steering Committees as standing committees. The conception of these bodies assisted teams I worked with to win several grants, which after being awarded, required those bodies to come alive. Of course, additional committees require additional staff time and costs in terms of meeting and communication logistics, minutes, reports, etc.; however, when those committees come together for full board membership meetings the synergy is unmistakable and the increase in board effectiveness is dynamic.

The due diligence of workforce development professional in fully developing a workforce development board and its committees can lead the lamenting cynic to say "those meetings are a waste of time." Similar complaints might be made about training conferences and other public meetings. While it can be true that despite our best intentions and greatest efforts, some meetings are indeed a waste of time; however, before the cynic pronounces a meeting dead, I would ask "why then, do you not lead?" The role of the workforce development professional is not to review a meeting, like a film critic, but to engage the attendees to fulfill the purposes of "convening."

One of the most fulfilling aspects of being a workforce development professional is achieving a state of competence where your passion, your enthusiasm, your imagination and your ideas can stimulate the development of those same gifts in others, not only to save an otherwise boring or useless meeting, but to collectively improve our profession and our professionals for the benefit of all of the constituencies that we serve.

A final word about meetings applies to internal staff meetings among board staff, WIOA grant recipient, sub-recipient fiscal agent and/or program staff. Those meetings should be well-planned in advance of convening, with an agenda and clear objectives in mind. To connect topics, teams and staff, I recommend the use of a "priority items matrix," through which a leader identifies the issues to be discussed, deliverable dates, status and planned outcomes. The meeting can be facilitated by a leader who might be subservient in the organization to superiors in the room, but who possesses the command of the issues necessary to explain them in the context of the full system. In my experience, system staff would prefer this level of structure and organization because it enhances teamwork, and esprit de corps, while helping them to understand how their sub-routines support and are supported by the system at large, thus leading to a more imaginative workforce development system.

Imaginative boards are effective boards whose impact may extend far and wide. WIOA provides workforce development professionals with the opportunities to position local boards to make an impact beyond the boundaries of their local workforce development area. While a truly effective board can make an impact on a national and indeed an international level, as well as on a state and local level, local boards must also engage in regional planning. This requirement is communicated in the WIOA citations below:

Section 107(d)(1) states:

"The local board, in partnership with the chief elected official for the local area involved, shall develop and submit a local plan to the Governor that meets the requirements in section 108. If the local area is part of a planning region that includes other local areas, the local board shall collaborate with the other local boards and chief elected officials from such other local areas in the preparation and submission of a regional plan as described in section 106(c)(2)."[5]

Section 106(c)(2)(A)(B)(C)(D)(E)(F)(G)(H) of WIOA states:

"The local boards and chief elected officials in each planning region described in subparagraph (B) or (C) of subsection (a)(2) shall engage in a regional planning process that results in—

---

[5] Public Law 113-128, Section 107(d)(1)

(A) the preparation of a regional plan, as described in paragraph (2);

(B) the establishment of regional service strategies, including use of cooperative service delivery agreements;

(C) the development and implementation of sector initiatives for in-demand industry sectors or occupations for the region;

(D) the collection and analysis of regional labor market data (in conjunction with the State);

(E) the establishment of administrative cost arrangements, including the pooling of funds for administrative costs, as appropriate, for the region;

(F) the coordination of transportation and other supportive services, as appropriate, for the region;

(G) the coordination of services with regional economic development services and providers; and

(H) the establishment of an agreement concerning how the planning region will collectively negotiate and reach agreement with Governor on local levels of performance for, and report on, the performance accountability measures described in section 116(c), for local areas or the planning region."[6]

While the required content of regional plans according to the letter of the law essentially speaks for itself, the spirit of the law is significant in that it recognizes that most economies are organized on a regional, rather than a local basis. This means that the significant industry sectors and clusters, the labor market, the demographics of the workforce, and transportation patterns are not constricted by geopolitical boundaries. Indeed, many state agencies are aligned according to regional and not local boundaries. Consequently, it makes sense that regional planning and regional plans include strategies for collaboration, communication and alignment among the local boards of the region. In some cases, regions cross state lines, but nevertheless bear the same characteristics of within-state regions, thus requiring the working relationship of local boards described above.

As the workforce development professional continues the trek up the mountain of system building, the establishment, maintenance and

---

[6] Public Law 113-128, Section 106(c)(2)(A)(B)(C)(D)(E)(F)(G)(H)

continuous improvement of the relationship among the local boards of a region again provides new opportunities for success. Regional initiatives are therefore another aspect of our work which, while grounded in the rules, offer the vast expanse of a blank page where the future of our region is limited only by our imaginations. Part of that opportunity exists within the realm of regional grants that become available on a federal and state level.

Under a productive regional collaboration model, with the caveat that each board maintains its own identity and autonomy, opportunities might exist, where feasible, to coordinate planning activities, create universal operational processes for business services and recruitment of participants, collaborate on job fairs, align supportive services, classroom-based training and work-based training programs, and advocate with a single voice. This working relationship positions the boards of the region to not only achieve optimum efficiencies, but to become more competitive in applying for regional grants.

In addition to collaborating with other boards of the region and the work of the local boards themselves, a critical element of the local workforce development system required by WIOA is the establishment of a program services delivery system. Section 107(d)(10)(A)(i)(ii) of WIOA includes among the functions of the local board the following requirement:

"Consistent with section 121(d), the local board, with the agreement of the chief elected official for the local area—

(i) shall designate or certify one-stop operators as described in section 121(d)(2)(A); and

(ii) may terminate for cause the eligibility of such operators."[7]

In addition to the function of selecting the one-stop operator, Section 121(a)(1)(2)(3) assigns additional, related tasks to the board:

"Consistent with an approved State plan, the local board for a local area, with the agreement of the chief elected official for the local area, shall

(1) develop and enter into the memorandum of understanding described in subsection (c) with one-stop partners;

---

[7] Public Law 113-128, Section 107(d)(10)(A)(i)(ii)

(2) designate or certify one-stop operators under subsection (d); and

(3) conduct oversight with respect to the one-stop delivery system in the local area...121(a)."[8]

Each individual partner program has the power to positively impact the entire workforce development system and, at the same time the system can positively impact each individual partner. The extent to which positive impacts might be achieved depend greatly on the extent to which we, as a community of workforce professionals seek to realize a vision of the system and its partners beyond compliance, beyond obtaining signatures on a document that Public Law 113-128 calls a "memorandum of understanding," within the realm of a truly sincere and productive collaboration. Thus, our goal as a group should be to forge a real partnership that shares the common goals of the WIOA legislation and other related objectives, to be defined regionally and locally. If we not only believe in this level of collaboration, but demonstrate through our actions that each individual partner is an important element of the system, that the system is an important part of each partner, then the purpose of creating the system in the first place will be far greater than offering a box for a program monitor to check. Instead, we will create the most effective use of partner resources possible for the good of the people we exist to serve. Section 121(b)(1)(A)(i)(ii)(iii)(iv)(v) of WIOA describes the roles and responsibilities of the partners of the system, as follows:

"(b) ONE-STOP PARTNERS.—

(1) REQUIRED PARTNERS.—

(A) ROLES AND RESPONSIBILITIES OF ONE-STOP PARTNERS.—

Each entity that carries out a program or activities described in subparagraph (B) in a local area shall—

(i) provide access through the one-stop delivery system to such program or activities carried out by the entity, including making the career services described in section 134(c)(2) that are applicable to the program or activities available at the one-stop centers (in addition to any other appropriate locations);

---

[8] Public Law 113-128, Section 121(a)(1)(2)(3)

(ii) use a portion of the funds available for the program and activities to maintain the one-stop delivery system, including payment of the infrastructure costs of one-stop centers in accordance with subsection (h);

(iii) enter into a local memorandum of understanding with the local board, relating to the operation of the one-stop system, that meets the requirements of subsection (c);

(iv) participate in the operation of the one-stop system consistent with the terms of the memorandum of understanding, the requirements of this title, and the requirements of the Federal laws authorizing the program or activities; and

(v) provide representation on the State board to the extent provided under section 101."[9]

Section 121(b)(1)(B)(i)(ii)(iii)(iv)(v)(vi)(viii)(ix)(x)(xi)(xii) of WIOA describes who the required partners are, as follows:

"(B) PROGRAMS AND ACTIVITIES.—The programs and activities referred to in subparagraph (A) consist of—

(i) programs authorized under this title;

(ii) programs authorized under the Wagner-Peyser Act (29 U.S.C. 49 et seq.);

(iii) adult education and literacy activities authorized under title II;

(iv) programs authorized under title I of the Rehabilitation Act of 1973 (29 U.S.C. 720 et seq.) (other than section 112 or part C of title I of such Act (29U.S.C. 732, 741);

(v) activities authorized under title V of the Older Americans Act of 1965 (42 U.S.C. 3056 et seq.);

(vi) career and technical education programs at the postsecondary level authorized under the Carl D. Perkins Career and Technical Education Act of 2006(20 U.S.C. 2301 et seq.);

(vii) activities authorized under chapter 2 of title II of the Trade Act of 1974 (19 U.S.C. 2271 et seq.);

(viii) activities authorized under chapter 41 of title 38, United States Code;

---

[9] Public Law113-128, Section 121(b)(1)(A)(i)(ii)(iii)(iv)(v)

(ix) employment and training activities carried out under the Community Services Block Grant Act (42 U.S.C. 9901 et seq.);

(x) employment and training activities carried out by the Department of Housing and Urban Development;

(xi) programs authorized under State unemployment compensation laws (in accordance with

applicable Federal law);

(xii) programs authorized under section 212 of the Second Chance Act of 2007 (42 U.S.C. 17532); and (xiii) programs authorized under part A of title IV of the Social Security Act (42 U.S.C. 601 et seq.), subject to subparagraph..."[10]

By requiring that these programs work together as partners within a one-stop delivery system, WIOA has created a powerful amalgamation of knowledge, resources, business relationships and funding. What can be fortunate or unfortunate for a local area, and ultimately, on a much larger scale, is how imaginative local boards are in designing those one-stop delivery systems. Those workforce development board leaders and planners who are limited by the narrow viewpoints might not leverage the full potential and realize the depth of opportunity of their workforce development system. Those who are passionate, enthused, imaginative and well-informed about their workforce development profession could enjoy unlimited potential and opportunities, providing they are able to create reciprocal characteristics among their partners.

Section 121(b)(2)(A) of WIOA describes additional partners:

"(2) ADDITIONAL PARTNERS.—

(A) IN GENERAL.—With the approval of the local board and chief elected official, in addition to the entities described in paragraph (1), other entities that carry out workforce development programs described in subparagraph

(B) may be one-stop partners for the local area and carry out the responsibilities described in paragraph (1)(A).

(B) PROGRAMS.—The programs referred to in subparagraph (A) may include—

(i) employment and training programs administered by the Social Security Administration, including the Ticket to Work and Self-

---

[10] Public Law 113-128, Section 121(b)(1)(B)(i)(ii)(iii)(iv)(v)(vi)(viii)(ix)(x)(xi)(xii)

Sufficiency Program established under section 1148 of the Social Security Act (42 U.S.C. 1320b–19);

(ii) employment and training programs carried out by the Small Business Administration;

(iii) programs authorized under section ;6(d)(4) of the Food and Nutrition Act of 2008 (7 U.S.C. 2015(d)(4));

(iv) work programs authorized under section 6(o) of the Food and Nutrition Act of 2008 (7 U.S.C. 2015(o));

(v) programs carried out under section 112 of the Rehabilitation Act of 1973 (29 U.S.C. 732);

(vi) programs authorized under the National and Community Service Act of 1990 (42 U.S.C. 12501 et seq.); and

(vii) other appropriate Federal, State, or local programs, including employment, education, and training programs provided by public libraries or in the private sector."[11]

From my perspective, the inclusion of this passage in the law seems underscore the clarion call from the framers to the workforce professional to think beyond the minimum mandates of the law and envision the depth and breadth of partnerships that will fulfill the needs of a local area, while at the same time realizing their own unique vision of a workforce development system.

In addition to day-to-day working relationships, an effective forum for the development of these relationships is the committee structure described above. In the meetings of those committees, the passion, enthusiasm, and imagination of the workforce professional must not only be evident, but those qualities must be accompanied by visibly unselfish leadership, dedication, knowledge, attention to detail, teamwork, cooperation and hard work. Those qualities often foster reciprocal behavior from the partner representatives, which results in the checking of egos at the door of entry. Once a general consensus and commitment is established to work together, a strong foundation for system-building can be laid, so that it might grow like a skyscraper, higher and higher, not just in size, but in quality too.

In addition to the relationships formed and the sincere commitment to cooperate achieved among the partner organizations, one of the most important connecting girders of this skyscraper is a

---

[11] Public Law 113-128, Section 121(b)(2)(i)(ii)(iii)(iv)(v)(vi)(vii)

universal information technology system. As you design your IT system, do not delegate management decisions to your IT experts, rather as a workforce system-builder, you should lead them with your workforce expertise to achieve your vision. For example, although many local one-stop delivery systems must participate in a larger state operated IT system, I recommend filling in blanks that might exist in the larger system with a locally-based infrastructure. To maximize the impact of this technology, envision a system where at the point of intake for any partner willing to participate, an electronic record will be created for each participant. Remember that WIOA Section 121(b)(1)(A)(i) cited above, includes among the roles and responsibilities of the partners the following requirement:

"...provide access through the one-stop delivery system to such program or activities carried out by the entity, including making the career services described in section 134(c)(2) that are applicable to the program or activities available at the one-stop centers (in addition to any other appropriate locations);"[12]

The word that stands out to me in that passage is "access." In the most passive sense, some might say that access might be limited to handing a participant a brochure, including the names of partners on signage or lists, or even less. However, on an active and helpful level, the participant is informed, to the extent appropriate, of all of the services available within the system, as a whole. I suggest that this information should be transmitted and marketed in multiple formats, and should accommodate individuals with disabilities and special populations appropriately.

These formats should include web sites, signage, collateral material, group and individual orientation and information sessions, video presentations, and any other tools that are effective. Clearly, this cross-informing, cross marketing process must be linked to your IT system. In addition, as the local IT system is populated with participant information, I believe that the details of that information should affect prompts that indicate the participants' eligibility, as appropriate for partner programs. At the appropriate interval, the eligibility and services available information should be shared with the partners (through confidentiality releases and information

---

[12] Public Law 113-128, Section 121(b)(1)(A)(i)

sharing agreements and in compliance with governing statutes and policies). As the participant progresses in partner programs and activities, that information should be available to the system partners as an individual record and as part of a summary reporting system.

Effective data collection, entry and reporting systems support a performance evaluation process for the local workforce development system. Such a process can help the local board to take a deep dive into the factors that affect the statutorily required performance indicators. This feature of local workforce development system infrastructure is particularly relevant under WIOA, which unlike its predecessors, measures the performance, not only of discreet programs, but also, of the "core programs" collectively.

The "core programs" are defined under WIOA Section 3(12) as follows:

(12) CORE PROGRAM.—The term "core programs" means a program authorized under a core program provision."[13]

A "core program provision" is defined under WIOA Section 3(13) as follows:

"(13) CORE PROGRAM PROVISION.—The term "core program provision" means—

(A) chapters 2 and 3 of subtitle B of title I (relating to youth workforce investment activities and adult and dislocated worker employment and training activities);

(B) title II (relating to adult education and literacy activities);

(C) sections 1 through 13 of the Wagner-Peyser Act (29 U.S.C. 49 et seq.) (relating to employment services); and

(D) title I of the Rehabilitation Act of 1973 (29 U.S.C. 20 et seq.), other than section 112 or part C of that title (29 U.S.C. 732, 741) (relating to vocational rehabilitation services)."[14]

Now that core programs share accountability under the performance indicators, collaboration in entering, reporting and organizing data has replaced silo funded performance management. The implication of this sea change in performance extends by common sense and also through management by objectives to the quality management

---

[13] Public Law 113-128, Section 3(12)

[14] Public Law 113-128, Section 3(13)(A)(B)(C)(D)

program of the entire workforce development system. It is the final step of evaluation that is included in a perpetual cycle of conceiving, building, and operating the workforce development system.

Chapter V
Serving Special Populations through Systems within Systems

The power of the partnerships described in Chapter IV grows a tree of low hanging fruit for systems to serve special populations. Several of the mandated federal funding streams required by WIOA under Section 121(b)(1)(B) are earmarked to special populations. For example, *"activities authorized under title V of the Older Americans Act of 1965 (42 U.S.C. 3056 et seq.),"*[15] are earmarked for older workers, *"programs authorized under title I of the Rehabilitation Act of 1973 (29 U.S.C. 720 et seq.),"*[16] are earmarked for individuals with disabilities, and *"programs authorized under part A of title IV of the Social Security Act (42 U.S.C. 601 et seq.),"*[17] are earmarked for public assistance recipients, etc. It would not be uncommon for a participant to be eligible under the requirements of all three of the above example funding streams.

The one-stop system provides the opportunity for the administrators of each of these programs to coordinate services to the participant, not only with each other, but also, with the system. As partners of the system, the partner organizations not only have the opportunity to collaborate in the different capacities of partner to partner, and as partner to system, but as partners who, in a sense, lead their own systems. To visualize this dynamic, imagine a family tree with branches that extend to succeeding branches. In the same sense, the one-stop system, through its partners, leverages the "partners of the partners." For this reason, it is important that workforce development professionals, particularly those in leadership and planning capacities, ensure that the board, its partner network and the one-stop system and its partners are fully familiar

---

[15] Public Law 113-128, Section 121(b)(1)(B)(v)
[16] Public Law 113-128, Section 121(b)(1)(B)(iv)
[17] Public Law 113-128, Section 121(b)(1)(B)(xiii)

with each other's resources and that those resources are fully leveraged in a coordinated manner. If this is accomplished, then job seekers within special populations served by the one-stop system will not only receive services that are universal to all customers, but also specialized services, as they access opportunities that will align with their individual needs. As discussed earlier, workforce development professionals should build the workforce development system on the foundation of a full intellectual command of the WIOA statute and regulations. Some of the cement poured into that foundation must include the knowledge of the resources available through the WIOA mandated and non-mandated partners, and their partners, as well. Non-mandated partners, but very important partners, can include libraries, the United Way, and many others.

In addition to the benefits derived from the sharing of resources among partners, the workforce development system can also benefit from the protocols and practices of their partners. For example, many innovative practices have been conceived of and implemented by organizations that serve individuals with disabilities. The U.S. Department of Labor Office of Disability and Employment Policy, aka "ODEP," has fostered a good deal of this innovation through grant projects and training. Projects such as the Disability Navigator and the Disability Employment Initiative have not only linked new "mini-partnerships" within the traditional one-stop system partnerships, but they have also connected services to individuals with disabilities to advanced business services strategies, such as sector partnerships. Several of the grant projects that I was fortunate to be involved with that originated with ODEP were examples of the creation of successful one-to-one services to customers that were preceded by well-designed visioning, strategic planning and infrastructure building on the part of the workforce board. With the proper partnerships, resources and access points in place, dedicated staff may collaborate as teams to achieve outstanding outcomes.

One example of a service protocol designed for individuals with disabilities that *crosses over* as an effective tool for other populations, is the practice of customized employment. According to ODEP, customized employment is defined as follows:

"Customized employment is a process for achieving competitive integrated employment or self-employment through a relationship between employee and employer that is personalized to meet the

needs of both. It is a universal strategy that benefits many people, including people with disabilities who might not have found success through other employment strategies. In 2014, customized employment was included in Title IV of the Workforce Innovation and Opportunity Act (WIOA) as a strategy under the definition of supported employment."[18]

The strategy of personalizing a job to meet the needs of both the employer and the employee is effective in conducting job development for almost any customer, but particularly those within special populations, such as older workers, youth, and more. Designing and implementing services for special populations presents an opportunity to light up the brain of the workforce development professional so that it reaches full capacity in the development of partnerships, creation of services to job seekers and businesses, all while maximizing the potential of workers.

---

[18] https:/dol.gov./agencies/odep/program-areas/customized-employment

Chapter VI
The System, Center, Program Paradox

In my view, one of the most important work products of a workforce development professional's toil should be the establishment, maintenance and continuous improvement of the WIOA "program." In this context, we are focusing on the part of the program that might be defined as "retail" services to job seekers. This is because, to the public at large, one-stop career centers are the most recognizable "face" of the local workforce development system. For that reason, most people encountered by workforce development professionals will perceive their jobs, and indeed, the function of the workforce development system, in the context of the "retail" services of the center. Those services were summarized earlier as "…interviewing and referring job seekers to jobs, enrolling job seekers into training programs, writing job orders…"

While it is true that in most instances, a high-quality one-stop career center and a high quality WIOA program should be a work product of a workforce development system, paradoxically, both the career center and the WIOA program would operate at reduced efficiency if workforce development leaders focused either exclusively, or too intensively on them to the partial or full exclusion of the system. A lack of appreciation for and attention to the system would inexorably result in the reduced efficiency, and possibly, the complete collapse of both the program and the center. Why would such an imbalance of appreciation and attention occur? It could be due to the oversimplification of what workforce development is in the modern age. I believe that this oversimplification springs from a misperception that exists in the public at a large. However, it could also exist within the minds of some workforce development leaders. If such a misperception prevails, then we need to recognize our own biases and work to improve our mindset.

    This change of our mindset should include fostering an appreciation of the larger system, beyond the retail level. Our understanding can be increased by reading and studying the WIOA law and its regulations and policy guidance. These disciplines can determine how well we comprehend and then implement progressive practices of workforce legislation. Unfortunately, a chasm might exist between those who develop and implement a vision of the system and those who under value the visioning and creative planning process. This chasm can be widened or narrowed based upon how well we market the system, how innovative our systems are, and how much we have kept pace with technological, legal and cultural developments affecting the workplace. We must also seize opportunities to get our message across, be it through the media, to elected officials, at board and other WIOA and non-WIOA meetings, and at a grass roots level in conversations with family, friends, businesses and job seeker customers, and partners. Some of these opportunities are an extension of the points made earlier about explaining what we do for a living, embracing our own professionalism, as well as developing and using an elevator speech to be used on many appropriate occasions. Note that the elevator speech should be appropriately modified for different audiences and be delivered in a natural and conversation manner.

In order to ensure a proper understanding of the balance between the WIOA system, center and program, let us begin by examining what the law tells us. Below are some informative citations, along with corresponding commentary. WIOA Section 121(d) (1) (2) (A) (B) (i) (ii) (iii) (iv) (v) (vi) (vii) (3) (4) (A) (B) (C) states:

"(d) ONE-STOP OPERATORS.—

(1) LOCAL DESIGNATION AND CERTIFICATION.—Consistent with paragraphs (2) and (3), the local board, with the agreement of the chief elected official, is authorized to designate or certify one-stop operators and to terminate for cause the eligibility of such operators.

(2) ELIGIBILITY.—To be eligible to receive funds made available under this subtitle to operate a one-stop center referred to in subsection (e), an entity (which may be a consortium of entities)—

(A) shall be designated or certified as a one-stop operator through a competitive process; and

(B) shall be an entity (public, private, or nonprofit), or consortium of entities (including a consortium of entities that, at a minimum, includes 3 or more of the one-stop partners described in subsection

(b)(1)), of demonstrated effectiveness, located in the local area, which may include—

(i) an institution of higher education;

(ii) an employment service State agency established under the Wagner-Peyser Act (29 U.S.C. 49

et seq.), on behalf of the local office of the agency;

(iii) a community-based organization, nonprofit organization, or intermediary;

(iv) a private for-profit entity;

(v) a government agency; and

(vi) another interested organization or entity, which may include a local chamber of commerce or other business organization, or a labor organization..."[19]

The above WIOA passage, like many others, contains what I believe might be interpreted as somewhat straight-forward instructions, which upon deeper analysis are profound in their conception and application. For example, while the above passage informs us that *"the local board, with the agreement of the chief elected official, is authorized to designate or certify one-stop operators and to terminate for cause the eligibility of such operators,"*[20] the processes of "designation," "certification" and "termination" are all subject to "eligibility." The section goes on to list the type of organizations that are eligible after citing the consequential qualifier *"shall be designated or certified as a one-stop operator through a competitive process."*[21] This qualifier is consequential from my perspective because, while the earlier portion of the passage assigns the power of the workforce development board, in agreement with the chief elected official, to designate, certify and terminate operators, designation and certification must be executed through a competitive process, i.e. a competitive procurement process, which seems to indicate that a contractual relationship must exist between the board and the one-stop operator, and if the board is not formally incorporated, also with its fiscal agent. As a contractor to the board and/or its fiscal agent, in keeping with the requirements of

---

[19] Public Law 113-128, Section 121 (d)(1)(2)(A)(B)(i)(ii)(iii)(iv)(v)(vi)(3)(4)(A)(B)(C)

[20] Ibid.

[21] Ibid.

competitive procurement, the board and its one-stop operator are indeed separate entities performing separate and discreet functions. Therefore, one-stop operators serve at the pleasure of the board. While the contracts between operators and board and/or its fiscal agent might not be performance-based contracts per se, it seems logical that performance must be a determining factor for the board to consider during the processes of re-designation and termination, as appropriate. From my perspective, as I back up, hover above and view the workforce development system from a bird's eye view, I believe that we should be able to perceive a "firewall" installed between any one-stop operator and the board. That implied firewall is a critical characteristic of modern workforce legislation, beginning with the Workforce Investment Act of 1998, Public 105-220[22] and continuing under WIOA.

The importance of including requirements that create such a firewall are due, in my opinion, at least in part, to the impact of the Government Performance and Results Act of 1993.[23] The contractual relationship, the firewall, and foundation of those elements in a pursuit of performance excellence in federal programs should all exist as critical building blocks in the visioning, planning and development processes undertaken by the board and its staff for the local workforce development system, the program and the center. Therefore, the paradox is again revealed in that the center and its operator are separated from the board in terms of the functions they perform, but closely connected as critical components of the same system. In this sense, the board is the driver of a proverbial car, which is the workforce development system, the one-stop operator is the computer that coordinates the fuel combustion and electrical functions of the engine, and the center is the engine. Without a properly functioning driver, computer or engine, the vehicle, or the system cannot operate. There is a distinction between these components; however, in that the driver has the option to amend or replace the computer or the engine, while the reverse cannot occur (at least, not yet). While the computer, i.e. the one-stop operator, and

---

[22] https://www.federalregister-gov/documents/2000/08/11/00-19985/workforce-investment-act
[23] https://www.govinfo.gov/content/pkg/STATUTE-107/pdf/STATUTE-107-Pg285.pdf

the engine, i.e. the one-stop career center, cannot replace the driver, i.e. the local board, the driver may be replaced by an owner, i.e., the chief elected official or the governor, who in turn represent the people.

The WIOA law in Section 121(e)(1)(A)(B)(C)(D)(E) states:

(e) ESTABLISHMENT OF ONE-STOP DELIVERY SYSTEM.—

(1) IN GENERAL.—There shall be established in each local area in a State that receives an allotment under section 132(b) a one-stop delivery system, which shall—

(A) provide the career services described in section 134(c)(2);

(B) provide access to training services as described in section 134(c)(3), including serving as the point of access to training services for participants in accordance with section 134(c)(3)(G);

(C) provide access to the employment and training activities carried out under section 134(d), if any;

(D) provide access to programs and activities carried out by one-stop partners described in subsection (b); and

(E) provide access to the data, information, and analysis described in section 15(a) of the Wagner-Peyser Act (29 U.S.C. 49l–2(a)) and all job search, placement, recruitment, and other labor exchange services authorized under the Wagner-Peyser Act (29 U.S.C. 49 et seq.).[24]

Notice that the above passage requires the establishment of a *"a one-stop delivery system,"*[25] but makes no mention of a bricks and mortar career center, while mentioning the phrase "access to" no less than four times. The intentional inclusion of the term "delivery system" and omission of a reference to a "bricks and mortar career center," combined with the stress on providing access to *"training services,"*[26] *employment and training activities,"*[27] *"programs and activities carried out by one-stop partners described in subsection (b);*[28] and *"provide access to the data, information, and analysis described in section 15(a) of the Wagner-Peyser Act (29 U.S.C. 49l–*

---

[24] Public Law 113-128, Section 121 (e)(1)(A)(B)(C)(D)(E)
[25] Ibid.
[26] Ibid.
[27] Ibid.
[28] Ibid.

2(a)) and all job search, placement, recruitment, and other labor exchange services authorized under the Wagner-Peyser Act (29 U.S.C. 49 et seq.)"[29] sends a clear message to me that the visioning, planning, development, and oversight processes of the board should be guided by a primary and overriding concern for leveraging the resources of its partners to serve customers in a manner in which those resources are most accessible and effective.

Once the concept of "access" is established, reference to a bricks and mortar center is made in Section 121(e)(2)(A)(B)(i)(ii)(I)(II)(C) as follows:

"(2) ONE-STOP DELIVERY.—The one-stop delivery system—

(A) at a minimum, shall make each of the programs, services, and activities described in paragraph (1) accessible at not less than 1 physical center in each local area of the State; and

(B) may also make programs, services, and activities described in paragraph (1) available—

(i) through a network of affiliated sites that can provide 1 or more of the programs, services, and activities to individuals; and

(ii) through a network of eligible one-stop partners—

(I) in which each partner provides 1 or more of the programs, services, and activities to such individuals and is accessible at an affiliated site that consists of a physical location or an electronically or technologically linked access point; and(II) that assures individuals that information on the availability of the career services will be available regardless of where the individuals initially enter the statewide workforce development system, including information made available through an access point described in subclause (I);

(C) may have specialized centers to address special needs, such as the needs of dislocated workers, youth, or key industry sectors or clusters; and (D) as applicable and practicable, shall make programs, services, and activities accessible to individuals through electronic means in a manner that improves efficiency, coordination, and quality in the delivery of one-stop partner services."[30]

After stating *"at a minimum, shall make each of the programs, services, and activities described in paragraph (1) accessible at not*

---

[29] Ibid.
[30] Public Law 113-128, Section 121 (e)(2)(A)(B)(i)(ii)(I)(II)(C)

less than 1 physical center in each local area of the State,"[31] the remainder of this passage provides opportunities for workforce development boards to creatively collaborate with partners to expand and improve customer "access,"[32] to connect the delivery system to the board's work related to *"key industry sectors or clusters,"* and to *"make programs, services, and activities accessible to individuals through electronic means in a manner that improves efficiency, coordination, and quality in the delivery of one-stop partner services"*[33]

The only partner organization that the law seems to mandate to be physically located in the bricks and mortar center is the provider of Wagner-Peyser services. This requirement is stipulated by WIOA Section 121(e)(3) as follows:

"Consistent with section 3(d) of the Wagner-Peyser Act (29 U.S.C. 49b(d)), and in order to improve service delivery, avoid duplication of services, and enhance coordination of services, including location of staff to ensure access to services in underserved areas, the employment service offices in each State shall be co-located with one-stop centers established under this title..."[34]

With this passage, the framers appear to be telling us that the co-location of Wagner-Peyser services are essential to the things they value and what they want local boards to value, including: access, non-duplication of services, and *"access to services in underserved areas."*[35]

Reflecting upon this section of WIOA should not lessen the attention we place on the characteristics of our "retail" operations. The career centers that we plan, design and operate should be accessible, technologically proficient, preferably on the cutting edge, welcoming, comfortable, customer-friendly, properly staffed and stocked with computers, assessment tools and systems, career

---

[31] Ibid.
[32] Ibid.
[33] Ibid.
[34] Ibid.
[35] Ibid.

libraries, collateral material, classrooms, workshops, audio visual systems, adaptive and accessible equipment and accommodations for individuals with disabilities and more.

Nevertheless, in our zeal to create and operate these high-quality physical centers, we must remember that they cannot fulfill the ambitious goals of a one-stop delivery system, without orbiting within the larger workforce development system. In this regard, the workforce development professional must intellectually navigate through the paradox of the board and its staff being separated by a firewall from the center and the program operations and staff, while at the same time being intrinsically linked in a seamless one-stop delivery system.

Chapter VII
Achieving Customer Satisfaction with Products That Melt

Almost everyone likes ice cream. If you do and you have treated yourself and perhaps your family to a trip to an old-fashioned ice cream parlor, your understanding of the difference between customer service and customer satisfaction related to ice cream will provide a good analogy for achieving customer satisfaction in the workforce development industry. After you order your favorite flavor, let us say on a cone, the person behind the counter will usually process your payment, fill the cone with the requested number of scoops, put on a topping and then hand you the cone. If all of that occurs, you have received customer service. We cannot determine whether or not you have attained customer satisfaction, unless and until we determine the answers to several questions, such as those listed below and perhaps more:

- How did you locate the ice cream parlor?
- Is it well known in the community?
- Did you hear about it through word of mouth?
- Did you discover it through a web site, or through social media?
- If you drove to this establishment, was it easy to find?
- Does its location offer convenient and efficient parking?
- Is its signage inviting and appropriate?
- What was your first impression when you entered the store?
- Is the facility clean?
- Is it accessible to individuals with disabilities?
- Was the staff courteous and professional?
- Did they seem to be passionate about their work?
- Did they project enthusiasm?
- Did they wear a name tag or other identification to make it clear that they were there to serve you?

- Were they dressed and presented in a manner that projects good health and hygiene for handling food, as well as appropriateness for the job they perform?
- Was the product selection sufficient?
- Was your order filled correctly?
- How long did you need to wait to be served?
- Did any part of your experience include an unexpected requirement on your part? For example, were you told to stand in a particular area after you placed your order, or while you were waiting?
- Was any action required of you that was even slightly inconvenient? For example, were you told that only cash would be accepted?
- Were all of your ancillary expectations met? For example, were there enough napkins, spoons and/or straws?
- Was there a comfortable place to sit and nice environment for you and your group that added to the experience while you ate the ice cream?
- How did the ice cream taste?
- Did it meet your expectations?
- Was there any after taste?
- Did it upset your stomach that night, or the next day?
- If anything did not meet your expectations that required an explanation or an accommodation by the staff, did they seem to respect your position as a customer?
- Would you patronize this business again?
- Would you be recognized as a repeat customer if you returned?
- Did the ice cream establishment follow-up on your visit in any way, such as with a coupon via snail or an email? Or, even with a phone call to determine your level of satisfaction?

If you are thinking, "all of this for an ice cream cone?" Obviously, the answer is yes and you knew that, but we sometimes do not stop to itemize the many complicated actions that lead to customer satisfaction, even in a simple service process.

Are these processes the same in the workforce industry? Yes, except that our products usually do not melt, or do they? If we think of our processes, particularly in one-stop career centers, as moments in our customers lives, in a sense, our products may be subject to melting away, forever, and never to return. This is because the moments may represent opportunities, when figurative planets are essentially aligned, when everything falls into place to fulfill the customer's goals, and thus achieve satisfaction. Conversely, other moments, such as when a poor first impression is made, or when inaccurate information is transmitted, or when information is withheld, when a deadline for a class enrollment is missed, when we fail to go the extra mile for lack of passion and enthusiasm, those important moments often cannot be recovered, and thus, we are not the professionals we aspire to be, and sadly, we fail.

Customer satisfaction with ice cream, workforce development, and indeed, all products that melt, is best achieved within a continually improving quality management program. Earlier, I referred to the Malcolm Baldrige principles. Using these principles, a quality management system may be created, sustained and constantly replenished. A critical element of these principles is customer-driven, fact-based, managerial decision-making. The design of an agile data collection and analysis system supports this process. The U.S. Department of Labor developed *Simply Better*,[36] a quality management initiative that included a system to collect data on both how important customers considered a service, as well as their level of satisfaction with the same service. This data is instructive when plotted on an axis graph.

Just like our products, which are prone to melting, customer satisfaction must be determined and evaluated on a timely and constant basis to ensure quality management and continuous improvement. While your quality management system should be robust and sophisticated, remember this, at the end of the day everything we do in the field of workforce development comes down to a one-to-one interaction with the customer. From that interaction we must ask a question that is so telling of the success. In a dramatic work, success is usually determined by whether or not the

---

[36] Training and Employment Information Notice No. 12-98, United States Department of Labor, October 8, 1998

protagonist achieved their goal. On the stage of workforce development, where the customer is the protagonist, the success of the workforce development professional is determined by the answer to the question "did the customer attain their intended goal?" If the answer is "no," for whatever reason, we failed. If the answer is "yes," everything we did to create and to operate the system was worth the effort, and the bonus is that not only was the customer fulfilled, but also, so was the workforce development professional. Enjoy your ice cream!

Chapter VIII
Career Services

Have you ever been sucked through a valve into an internal combustion engine? Neither have I, but it does not sound like a fun experience. It is a process referred to as "intake," which ironically is the same name that many local workforce development systems give to their welcoming process, which is essentially the starting point for career services. Kudos to the many leaders who have created innovative, customer-friendly processes, for welcoming customers. Those processes must include a degree of administration and bureaucracy, but the most progressive ones add value incrementally and avoid repetition throughout the customer's contact with the system. Progressive welcoming processes are adept at managing customer satisfaction with products that melt. They understand that seemingly inconsequential and innocent service failures, even those that might only exist in the eye of the customer, can solidify customer impressions, forming intractable opinions of us that will haunt us as we attempt to serve and satisfy them.

To navigate the welcoming process successfully, and indeed, to construct effective service protocols from the point of customer entry to customer exit, workforce development system designers must master a dance that balances compliance with value. Both compliance requirements and the value that can be added are described in WIOA Section 134 (c)(2). The opening passage of Section 134 (c)(2)(A) informs us that the career services it defines are reserved for adults and dislocated workers by stating the following:

"(A) SERVICES PROVIDED.—Funds described in paragraph (1) shall be used to provide career services, which shall be available to individuals who are adults or dislocated workers through the one-stop delivery system..."[37]

---

[37] Public Law 113-128, Section 134(c)(2)(A)

The same section goes on to say...

"and shall, at a minimum, include—

(i) determinations of whether the individuals are eligible to receive assistance under this subtitle;

(ii) outreach, intake (which may include worker profiling), and orientation to the information and other services available through the one-stop delivery system;"[38]

In my view, the above passage shuts down the argument made by some that a progressive welcoming system should be unencumbered by any eligibility requirements at all. It is significant that the determination of eligibility is positioned first on the list of career services. From a logical perspective, this positioning seems to be telling us that because only eligible adults and dislocated workers can receive career services, welcoming processes should be designed to determine eligibility as early in the process as possible. This requirement presents a customer service and a "first impression" challenge to service providers because they are by statute mandated to present the new customer with at least some level of bureaucracy during the period when the customer's first impression is being formed. However, as we discussed in the Introduction to this book, accepted with the proper mindset, challenges may give birth to opportunities.

In order to develop the proper mindset, workforce development professionals should understand some essential truths. To begin with, eligibility determination is by statute a service and, as such, by completing this process with the customer, albeit unavoidably bureaucratic on some level, the staff person conducting the determination process is indeed providing a service to the customer. Without receiving this service, the customer cannot receive the many other effective career, training, and supportive services that are necessary to fulfill the customer's goals. Understanding these facts, the staff person should not ever attempt to devalue the eligibility determination service in the customer's eyes by complaining about it, acting guilty about it, or leading the customer to believe that some bogeyman invented and/or enforces it. Taking these missteps might be a temptation for the staff person, perhaps motivated by the staff

---

[38] Public Law 113-128, Section 134(c)(2)(A)(i)(ii)

person's own biases, such as a belief that the eligibility should not be required. Or, it could be motivated by the staff person's fear of conflict with the customer, since some people who seek services balk at the idea of sharing and/or documenting personal information.

A power struggle between the customer and the staff person who is tasked with determining eligibility is of course counterproductive to the customer and everyone involved. It is more likely that such a struggle could emerge if the staff person undermines the process, is unsure of its purpose, or undersells its purpose. In addition to properly training welcoming staff to articulate the reason the eligibility that must be determined, system leaders should reinforce the information transmitted during the eligibility determination interview with additional methods of communication. These additional methods might include disseminating a positive message about the process on the system web site, in collateral material, during rapid response meetings, in group orientation meetings, and more.

Another medium for disseminating this message is to produce an orientation film. Once again, the "challenge" of transmitting the proper message, could indeed create an opportunity for the system to rise to a higher level of professionalism. A film is an excellent opportunity to solidify the brand and image of the system. Visual media has the potential to form many positive impressions among a variety of customers and stakeholders, beyond job seekers, to businesses, elected officials, partners, funders, and the public at large. The orientation film can serve as a marketing tool to expand the footprint of the system, heretofore constrained by the walls of a physical orientation room within a career center to the much wider audience of the internet.

It is incumbent upon workforce professionals to walk in the shoes of the customers that they serve. In the Chapter entitled "Enthusiasm" we described a professional career counselor as follows: "Such an individual must be the expert, or at least passionately desire to evolve into the expert that their customers, deserve and expect." If we are to walk in the shoes of our customers, then we are to understand that those shoes took many exhausting steps before coming to rest before us. We will also understand that the customers who don such well-trodden footwear will, in many cases, feel they have reached the pinnacle point of their journey, perhaps not of career and economic success, but at the very least, for the help they need to achieve those goals. Without the proper information, customers might, as they would in any similar field of endeavor, wander aimlessly almost timelessly down many false, dark and labyrinthine corridors, with the hopes and dreams contained in their soles, and indeed their souls, wearing away more and more of both with each step that leads, not to the light, but to a wall of stone.

It is an unfortunate but persistent fact that at the perceived pinnacle point of their quest for help, when they are expecting to discuss career goals and services available, they must take a detour into the administrative crevice of eligibility determination, which includes the process of data element validation. While the expectations of the customer do not relieve us of our statutory responsibility, part of that responsibility is to guide the customer to the service access points that lie just beyond the dimmed pathways of frustration and ignorance of how the system can help them. The staff person, who is charged with the helpful, compassionate and important task of encountering the customer at this juncture, and then guiding them ever higher, cannot be weak of heart. In fact, this is a precise moment when passion, enthusiasm, expertise, and the ability to help the customer must transcend mere good intentions with the application of workforce development professionalism. This is not the moment for staff to trip on the brier of uncertainty or disloyalty to the system.

We have established that eligibility determination is a service to the customer, and a gateway to many more valuable services and resources. Therefore, there should be no shame, doubt, hesitation, or passive-aggressiveness in performing it. Indeed, there should be no statements from staff along the lines of "I don't know why they make me ask you for all of this." Customers will spot even the subtlest indicators of cynicism, weakness, or disloyalty in the person who is supposed to be serving them. Thus, the workforce professional needs to not only believe in the task being performed, whether it is eligibility determination, or even negotiation of a contract with an employer for on-the-job training, but must also execute such tasks with passion and enthusiasm. On the other hand, staff conducting this task must not install themselves, or by extension the system or program they represent, as authoritarian gatekeepers who essentially create the impression that the customer must cooperate because "I" or "we say so." If we truly walk in the shoes of others, if we empathize with them, if we place ourselves in their position, then we will realize how much more motivated our customers will be, if they understand why we are conducting eligibility determination. If we conduct that task with respect for their dignity in a confident professional manner, not only are we abiding by sound morals and ethics, we will garner more cooperation and operate more successful programs. That success will be defined, not only by customer satisfaction, but also by fulfillment of customer goals and improved performance outcomes for the workforce development system.

The one-stop system welcoming process should extend to a host of outreach activities, including Rapid Response meetings for workers affected by the Worker Adjustment Retraining Notification (WARN) Act. Presentations made by one-stop system staff at these meetings should be designed and delivered in a manner sensitive to the plight of workers who are facing, or have already experienced layoffs. In my experience, the first priority in the minds of individuals in this situation is to determine how they are going to continue to support themselves after the layoff. For this reason, it is a good idea for the meeting planners to schedule presentations by the employer's severance and benefits officers regarding separation resources, and appropriate staff regarding the process for applying for and the conditions for receiving unemployment insurance, to precede discussions of WIOA-funding training and re-employment services.

Immediately after the task of eligibility determination, Section 134(c)(2)(A)(iii) requires the following services:

"(iii) initial assessment of skill levels (including literacy, numeracy, and English language proficiency), aptitudes, abilities (including skills gaps), and supportive service needs;"[39]

Key to this service is the modifier "initial," which implies that more in-depth assessment will follow in the proper sequence of the service protocol. However, although the word initial implies a more cursory approach, without laying the proper foundation for the purpose of these services, it can be perceived by the customer as the highest

---

[39] Public Law 113-128, Section 134(c)(2)(A)(iii)

hurdle of the system to pass, and consequently, result in some hostility and recalcitrance by the customer more than any part of the career services process. Such a response might occur, among dislocated workers, in particular, who might feel that stating their qualifications, or submitting a resume, or completing application describing their experience and/or education alone should suffice to move the staff person to immediately connect them with a job opening or a training program that is commensurate with their career goals and their salary expectations.

Customers operating from this perspective might not understand the purpose of assessment, feeling that their qualifications should speak for themselves; while in reality this is rarely the case. It is the job of the workforce development system to help the customer to understand that the process of becoming employed, especially that of a dislocated worker becoming reemployed, often requires the acquisition of new credentials and skills and new methods of marketing those skills and credentials. This is because the workplace is continually changing and those changes affect the marketability of job seekers. In fact, in some cases, the fact that an individual lost pace with those changes could be the reason that they transitioned from the status of an employed worker to a dislocated worker.

The constant forces of change in the workplace have accelerated geometrically in the modern era. This rapidity of change mirrors the exponentially faster rate of discovery, invention and development as compared to one hundred years ago and further back. Clearly, new technology is emerging at a faster and faster rate, which impacts on how work is performed. In addition, as the Introduction stated, "a sequence of events, from the global to the local level, along with other factors, such as societal evolution, cultural changes and technological advancements which are continuing to chip away at the world as we perceive it," change the workplace and our perceptions of it every day.

In view of the dynamics of change, without explaining and reinforcing the importance of aligning job seeker credentials and skills with <u>current</u> labor market demands, welcoming systems will be vulnerable to dissatisfaction among customers who might be insulted to take a math or reading test, even if ascertaining their level of proficiency is necessary to determine if they might meet the entry qualifications for a course that they wish to be enrolled into.

Of course, a discerning and sensitive career counselor should also understand that there might be some internal fear mixed in with a job seeker's external bluster. Indeed, our welcoming systems need, not only to transmit pertinent and prescient information, they must be designed to accommodate the psychological barriers faced by our customers. The challenge to present this information properly, once again, may be transformed into an opportunity for better services and a more successful system. For example, labor market information should be woven consistently into the customer's experience, including during information or orientation sessions, rapid response meetings, assessment and beyond. Being tethered to labor market information early on in all of our interactions with job seeker establishes the proper direction for our collaboration with the job seeker. Many customers perceive the welcoming process as being akin to applying for a job. Some customers will act as if they need to impress us with their qualifications to get the best service. Putting a best foot forward is of course a good idea in any interview, obviously in a hiring situation, but also in a helping interview. However, the workforce system interviewer should set the proper tone by explaining what is currently in demand, then what follows will be an alignment of the job seeker's goals, qualifications and next action steps with the real demands of labor market. Without setting the proper tone, the customer is left only with the impression that their "best foot forward" is not good enough.

Beyond the welcoming process, Section 134 (c)(2)(A)(iv) constructs an arena of further challenges and opportunities in with the following passage:

"(iv) labor exchange services, including—

(I) job search and placement assistance and, in appropriate cases, career counseling, including—

(aa) provision of information on in-demand industry sectors and occupations; and

(bb) provision of information on nontraditional employment;"[40]

Despite the sequence of *"information on in-demand industry sectors and occupations"* after eligibility determination, I

---

[40] Public Law 113-128, Section 134(c)(2)(A)(iv)(I)(aa)(bb)

recommend that this sharing of labor market information should, as stated above begin as early as possible. The nature of the information should include federal and state statistical projections, along data shared through a variety of media from the employers themselves. This includes company web sites, X, Linked-In and other social media. It is very effective to orient customers to delve into these sources during group and individual welcoming sessions, as well as to foster their research of these sources and others, particularly those that are industry-driven on a daily basis. In addition, the U.S. Department of Labor Employment and Training Administration, the New York State Department of Labor, and other organizations provide access to several tools that help connect labor market information with initial assessment in a manner that can heighten customer understanding of the need to align their skills with the labor market.

WIOA Section 134(c)(2)(A)(iv)(II) states further:

"(II) appropriate recruitment and other business services on behalf of employers, including small employers, in the local area, which services may include services described in this subsection, such as providing information and referral to specialized business services not traditionally offered through the one-stop delivery system;"[41]

These services will be explored in depth in the chapter entitled "Moving Beyond Business Services..."

WIOA Section 134(c)(2)(A)(v) then states:

"(v) provision of referrals to and coordination of activities with other programs and services, including programs and services within the one-stop delivery system and, in appropriate cases, other workforce development programs;"[42]

This is of course a central mission of the one-stop career center system. Section 134(c)(2)(A)(vi) revisits labor market information again with the passage below, which underscores the importance of tethering it to the welcoming process.

"(vi) provision of workforce and labor market employment statistics information, including the provision of accurate

---

[41] Public Law 113-128, Section 134(c)(2)(A)(iv)(II)
[42] Public Law 113-128, Section 134(c)(2)(A)(v)

information relating to local, regional, and national labor market areas, including—
(I) job vacancy listings in such labor market areas;
(II) information on job skills necessary to obtain the jobs described in subclause (I); and
(III) information relating to local occupations in demand and the earnings, skill requirements,
and opportunities for advancement for such occupations;"[43]

As this section continues it requires that performance information be shared with the customer, as described below:

"(vii) provision of performance information and program cost information on eligible providers of training services as described in section 122, provided by program, and eligible providers of youth workforce investment activities described in section 123, providers of adult education described in title II, providers of career and technical education activities at the postsecondary level, and career and technical education activities available to school dropouts, under the Carl D. Perkins Career and Technical Education Act of 2006 (20 U.S.C. 2301 et seq.), and providers of vocational rehabilitation services described in title I of the Rehabilitation Act of 1973 (29 U.S.C. 720 et seq.);
(viii) provision of information, in formats that are usable by and understandable to one-stop center customers, regarding how the local area is performing on the local performance accountability measures described in section 116(c) and any additional performance information with respect to the one-stop delivery system in the local area;"[44]

I believe that an ideal way to share this information is through well-presented collateral material and/or reports that market the attributes and importance of the system, while, where possibly communicating about its successes, defined by valid metrics. The inclusion of the services below in this section is an inexorable component of the "one-stop" approach.

"(ix)(I) provision of information, in formats that are usable by and understandable to one-stop center customers, relating to the

---

[43] Public Law 113-128, Section 134(c)(2)(A)(vi)(I)(II)(III)
[44] Public Law 113-128, Section 134(c)(2)(A)(vii)(viii)

availability of supportive services or assistance, including child care, child support, medical or child health assistance under title XIX or XXI of the Social Security Act (42 U.S.C. 1396 et seq. and 1397aa et seq.), benefits under the supplemental nutrition assistance program established under the Food and Nutrition Act of 2008 (7 U.S.C. 2011 et seq.), assistance through the earned income tax credit under section 32 of the Internal Revenue Code of 1986, and assistance under a State program for temporary assistance for needy families funded under part A of title IV of the Social Security Act (42 U.S.C.601 et seq.) and other supportive services and transportation provided through funds made available under such part, available in the local area; (II) referral to the services or assistance described in subclause (I), as appropriate;"[45]

The section also requires that career services include the following:
"(x) provision of information and assistance regarding filing claims for unemployment compensation;
(xi) assistance in establishing eligibility for programs of financial aid assistance for training and education programs that are not funded under this Act;"[46]

In the following passage the requirements for both in-depth assessment and in- career services are stated:
"(xii) services, if determined to be appropriate in order for an individual to obtain or retain employment, that consist of—
(I) comprehensive and specialized assessments of the skill levels and service needs of adults and dislocated workers, which may include—
(aa) diagnostic testing and use of other assessment tools; and (bb) in-depth interviewing and evaluation to identify employment barriers and appropriate employment goals;
(II) development of an individual employment plan, to identify the employment goals, appropriate achievement objectives, and appropriate combination of services for the participant to achieve the employment goals, including providing information on eligible

---

[45] Public Law 113-128, Section 134(c)(2)(A)(ix)(I)
[46] Public Law 113-128, Section 134(c)(2)(A)(x)(xi)

providers of training services pursuant to paragraph (3)(F)(ii), and career pathways to attain career objectives;"[47]

The next part of the same section describes a series of products and services to be offered by the one-stop delivery system, including group services.

"(III) group counseling;
(IV) individual counseling;
(V) career planning;
(VI) short-term prevocational services, including development of learning skills, communication skills, interviewing skills, punctuality, personal maintenance skills, and professional conduct, to prepare individuals for unsubsidized employment or training;
(VII) internships and work experiences that are linked to careers;
(VIII) workforce preparation activities;
(IX) financial literacy services, such as the activities described in section 129(b)(2)(D);
(X) out-of-area job search assistance and relocation assistance; or
(XI) English language acquisition and integrated education and training programs..."[48]

Finally, "follow-up" services are required, as stated below:
(xiii) follow-up services, including counseling regarding the workplace, for participants in workforce investment activities authorized under this subtitle who are placed in unsubsidized employment, for not less than 12 months after the first day of the employment, as appropriate."[49]

The statutory requirements for career services are augmented in greater detail by Training and Employment Guidance Letter (TEGL) Number 19-16, issued by the United Department of Labor (UDSOL) Employment and Training Administration (ETA) on March 1, 2017. This document organizes career services into three types, including

---

[47] Public Law 113-128, Section 134(c)(2)(A)(xii)(I)(aa)(bb)(II)
[48] Public Law 113-128, Section 134(c)(2)(A)(xii)(III)((IV)(V)(VI)(VII)(VIII)(IX)(X)(XI)
[49] Public Law 113-128, Section 134(c)(2)(A)(xiii)

"basic service, individualized services and follow-up services."[50] Basic services are described as follows:

"Basic career services are universally accessible and must be made available to all individuals seeking employment and training services in at least one comprehensive American Job Center per local area. Generally, these services involve less staff time and involvement and include services such as: eligibility determinations, initial skill assessments, labor exchange services, provision of information on programs and services, and program referrals. These services may be provided by both the Adult and Dislocated Worker programs, as well as by the Employment Service. Individualized Career Service."[51]

Individualized services are described as follows:

"Individualized career services must be provided to participants after American Job Center staff determine that such services are required to retain or obtain employment, consistent with any applicable statutory priorities. Generally, these services involve significant staff time and customization to each individual's need. Individualized career services include services such as: specialized assessments, developing an individual employment plan, counseling, work experiences (including transitional jobs), etc."[52]

The requirement that these services *"must be provided to participants after American Job Center staff determine that such services are required to retain or obtain employment"*[53] tells me that program operators must have a consistent, well-documented criteria in place for making this determination, such as an attestation form. The description of individualized services concludes with the statement below:

"Local Workforce Development Boards (WDBs) must identify the assessments to be used to determine eligibility, and ensure eligibility determination procedures are consistent with state policies.

---

[50] Training and Employment Guidance Letter Number 19-16 Operating Guidance for Workforce Innovation and Opportunity Act, Employment and Training Advisory System, United States Department of Labor, March 1, 2017
[51] Ibid.
[52] Ibid.
[53] Ibid.

American Job Center staff may use recent previous interviews, evaluations, or assessments by partner programs to determine if individualized career services would be appropriate. These services generally will be provided by the Adult and Dislocated Worker programs, although it may be appropriate for the Employment Service to provide some of these services."[54]

The TEGL augments that statutory definition of follow-up services with this passage:

"States and local areas must provide follow-up services for adults and dislocated worker participants who are placed in unsubsidized employment, for up to 12 months after the first day of employment. States and local areas must establish policies that define what are considered to be appropriate follow-up services, as well as policies for identifying when to provide follow-up services to participants. One type of follow-up service highlighted in WIOA is to provide individuals counseling about the work place. Follow-up services do not extend the date of exit in performance reporting; for more information on performance reporting see TEGL 10-16."[55]

The requirement to conduct follow-up services is consistent with requirements of the WIOA performance indicators, i.e., two and four quarters after exit. An effective system for improving performance indicator outcomes and complying with the requirement stated in TEGL 19-16 to conduct follow-up services for adults and dislocated workers is to integrate post-program data collection activities with follow-up services. This integration creates a process in which staff are not simply asking exited customers for statistical reporting information, but also providing useful services to help those customers to obtain and retain employment and achieve wage gains. Moreover, it enhances customer satisfaction in that it demonstrates long-term commitment and concern.

---

[54] Ibid.
[55] Ibid.

Chapter IX
Performance Leadership

Human nature drives man in any endeavor, especially in defeat, to ponder what might have been. Such musings are often poignant, romantic and poetic in their appraisal of the ironic and sometimes tragic, often bittersweet, will of fate. If only I had left for work at the usual time, I would have avoided an accident. If only we had met under different circumstances, a romance might have blossomed. If only the umpire didn't make that bad call...and on and on we go.

In this chapter we will discuss performance standards in the competitive endeavor of workforce development. Local workforce development boards and program operators do not design the standards, or create the rules in which they are applied. There are always mitigating circumstances that are often unforeseen, and sometimes these circumstances seem to be cruel and unfair. While there are occasional dispensations granted, workforce development professionals are expected to display integrity in reporting and to accept the consequences of those reports. Whether those consequences are positive or negative, providing that they do not result in reorganization, i.e., going out of business, they are opportunities for learning and continuous improvement.

No matter what the endeavor might be, while not excusing ourselves from accountability, consolation may arise from learning from our mistakes. This analysis will allow us to learn lessons and improve, which are key elements of never giving up. At the same time, we must ultimately ground ourselves in reality, particularly when the rules for calculating the statistic, the record, or in the case of a workforce development program, performance outcomes, are established by someone other than the performer. This is true in the case of workforce development program performance, even though the standards are "negotiated." This is because acceptance or rejection of the standards proposed by the performer fall under the auspices of a higher authority than the program operator, i.e., the United States Department of Labor for states, and the state authority for local boards.

The sturdy practices of augmenting standards, tracking independent statistics, publicizing locally established reports, and even maintaining locally controlled management information systems, might support good quality management, but the existence of those standards, data and systems does not erase the consequences of failing to attain standards that are calculated based upon a statutory formula. This point was driven home to me while attending a performance meeting convened by an oversight agency. The agency was reviewing local performance standard results, sort of like openly sharing report card results with the whole class at school. One local representative, embarrassed by the poor performance of his local area and trying to bargain himself and his organization away from the consequences of its failures, argued to the lead agency officer, "You don't understand, those are not our numbers."

To which the officer responded, "That's funny, because guess what? They are!"

At a similar meeting, a local representative argued that the local operator had far surpassed all of the negotiated performance goals, except for one which they failed rather miserably. The oversight officer who was running the meeting explained that if his child came home from school with a report card of straight "A's," except for one "F," he would be extremely unhappy.

Once, at a training conference, a presenter took this report card grading analogy a little further with this example. Let us say that the goal for a performance indicator is established for an entered employment rate and the goal for that rate is 60%. We will need to factor in that attainment of the standard, by statute, is achieved if the operator attains 80% of the 60% goal. To illustrate, if the operator reports that 48 participants out of 100 who exited from the program entered employment, because 60 out of 100 is 60%, 80% of 60 participants is 48 participants, thus, the standard is achieved. In this example, a local area can report to its constituents, including its chief elected officials, its board of directors, its customers, the public at large, even to the press that it has attained the standard. This same "success" could be reported for all of its federal-required standards. However, as is so often the case when dealing with statistics, the devil is in the details. Again, using a school report card analogy, the goal of 60% might equate to passing a course, i.e. a grade of "C." Had the outcome been 70 out of 100, which is 1.17% of the goal of 60%, the grade might equate to a "B." Had the outcome been 80 out of 100, which is 133% of the goal of 60%, the grade would have been an "A." Conversely, an outcome of 47 out 100, which is 78.3% and less than the minimum or "C" passing grade, might be graded as a "D." This means that the outcome of 48 participants who entered employment out of a universe of 100, the outcome that could technically be shouted from the rooftops as a success, is the difference of only one participant above a grade level of D (i.e. 47 participants). The outcome would not have to go much lower to be an "F."

In case there is any doubt, the above illustration is offered to you with the understanding that the majority placements or "entered-employments" are hard fought, well-deserved victories achieved by hard-working customers and workforce development professionals. Moreover, given the severe barriers faced by many of the job seekers we serve, a majority percentage means that, more often than not, we are making a positive difference in people's lives. And yet, from the perspective of an opportunity for continuous improvement and the desire to achieve excellence, we need to view our performance objectively and realistically. There is danger in publicly celebrating victories without qualification. In my view, our continued funding and survival essentially come down to a two-page report card. One page pertains to our fiscal operations and the other is the extent that we attain federally-required performance standards.

Surpassing performance goals and achieving excellence are outcomes grounded in our previous discussions of passion, enthusiasm, customer satisfaction and imagination, but our passion and enthusiasm should not alter our perception of reality. The bridge between our outcomes and our practices begins with the intellectual engagement of staff by leaders. When it comes to making this cerebral connection, leaders must understand how deeply to wade into the dark waters of performance data. Performance leadership is a delicate operation which can make or break success. Your leadership style might improve or hinder the performance of your system. In this regard, there are certain styles to avoid. For example, someone who proudly proclaims, I don't get involved in all of that, my (insert the name of a subordinate job title) figures all of that out. My question to this type of leader would be "really, then what do you do?" By delegating out of a belief that certain tasks or bodies of knowledge are above or below them, or that they are a distraction to the real job, not only are they not fulfilling their role, indeed, in a workforce development system, they are missing an opportunity to chart a course for success that is comparative to having a sixth sense and not using it.

In my travels, I witnessed this phenomenon on several occasions. One example was the leader of a large agency during the period when computer automation was expanding geometrically. The leader hired an intern to deal what he perceived to be the bothersome and relatively minor detail of automating the entire operation. Ultimately, this leader was actually delegating management decisions to the intern, erroneously assuming that those decisions only applied to some dark and mysterious world of computer operations and not the larger system. The successful performance leader must balance a big picture view with a command for, but not an obsession with details, while stimulating intellectual curiosity and emotional involvement among the staff. From this orientation, the following is an "argument" for performance through which the minds and hearts of staff may be engaged.

The first primary indicator of performance cited in the WIOA statute is stated below:

"The percentage of participants, who are in unsubsidized employment during the second quarter after exit from the program;"[56]

At a glance, it would seem that the job of public-facing staff, such as a career counselor or job placement specialist, is to help customers to get and keep jobs, which by itself is a laudable profession. Nonetheless, the workforce development staff leaders, and all of their constituencies would be better served to understand that the workforce development system does even more. I have argued that performance excellence depends in part on the intellectual engagement of staff.

---

[56] Public Law 113-128, Section 116(b)(2)(I)

One way to achieve that engagement is to lead them to perceive their role in the context of the stated purposes of the WIOA legislation, as cited below:

"The purposes of the Workforce Innovation and Opportunity Act are the following:

"(1) To increase, for individuals in the United States, particularly those individuals with barriers to employment, access to and opportunities for the employment, education, training, and support services they need to succeed in the labor market.

(2) To support the alignment of workforce investment, education, and economic development systems in support of a comprehensive, accessible, and high-quality workforce development system in the United States.

(3) To improve the quality and labor market relevance of workforce investment, education, and economic development efforts to provide America's workers with the skills and credentials necessary to secure and advance in employment with family-sustaining wages and to provide America's employers with the skilled workers the employers need to succeed in a global economy.

(4) To promote improvement in the structure of and delivery of services through the United States workforce development system to better address the employment and skill needs of workers, jobseekers, and employers.

(5) To increase the prosperity of workers and employers in the United States, the economic growth of communities, regions, and States, and the global competitiveness of the United States... [57]

The reader can either view those stated purposes apathetically, cynically, or idealistically, and by extension, the reader can view the role of the workforce development professional in the same way. Most of us have been advised from an early age to believe in ourselves and to respect ourselves, no matter what others might think or say. I would argue that this belief, and indeed this self-respect cannot be achieved for the workforce professional, unless they view the role of WIOA and other programs that they operate idealistically. That is not to say one cannot criticize legislative concepts and assumptions, or find fault with operational tactics. The trick is to pair

---

[57] Public Law 113-128, Section 2(1)(2)(3)(4)(5)(6)

those negative apprehensions with positive, well thought out alternatives. Encouraging staff to "think" about their jobs in this cerebral, yet passionate and enthusiastic fashion might elevate their individual and collective performance, and by extension the outcomes of the programs they operate.

I believe that the best approach to training workforce staff is to attempt to establish a firm foundation in their minds of the historical role of workforce development, the big picture of impact of these programs on business, the economy and the quality of life before targeting micro functions. This approach might be criticized with the reproach of "they don't need to know all that," or "that has nothing to do with their job." However, workforce leaders should understand that perceptions of workers and work places should exist as an ideal for others to follow and not illustrate humanity at its most inhumane. Therefore, I would challenge leaders to foster an appreciation among their workers for the importance of the programs they operate and to take pride in themselves as the most important resource, the human resource, in delivering those programs. That is not to say that workers should be simply granted a false sense of pride for the very fact that they are deployed in a career center. In fact, another critical concept that should be conveyed early on during staff training, and indeed as a reminder for veteran workers, is that most of us have been, or could be in the place of the customers we serve, including both job seekers and aspiring businesses.

As stated earlier, a brief encounter with a customer can dramatically change their life for better and for worse. In this sense, all workforce development professionals, including leaders and behind the scenes planners and fiscal staff, have a tremendous responsibility to create the most effective services possible through their individually assigned tasks. Being in awe of the importance of their work should not put them in awe of themselves, but rather give them an appreciation of the opportunity they have been given to do good, which is perhaps the greatest fulfillment any career can offer. While staff should view their roles through an intellectual lens and feel great pride in their work, they must earn the respect of their customers, leaders and other constituencies. To do so they must accept evaluations of their performance in a manner that is balanced with the solid foundation of positive self-esteem and a sincerely held desire to help. Based on our understanding that to "attain" a negotiated performance indicator goal is akin to earning a grade of "C," the true goal of a workforce development professional must be to "surpass" goals, hopefully by a sufficient margin to attain an "A." Even after attaining that hard won "A," our understanding of continuous improvement informs us that we should perpetually attempt to improve upon "A" after "A" and even "A+" after "A+."

The WIOA Primary Indicators of Performance indicators, which are cited in the WIOA statute at Section 116 (b), are provided in italics below, along with suggestions in bold for surpassing the goals negotiated for these indicators.

<u>Adults and Dislocated Workers</u>

<u>"Indicator</u>:

(I) the percentage of program participants who are in unsubsidized employment during the second quarter after exit from the program;"[58]

<u>Suggestions</u>:

In my experience, local workforce development boards often do not receive reports of their outcomes under the Primary Indicators of Performance until after the state has calculated employment outcomes for exiters based upon unemployment insurance earnings records. The state oversight agency makes these calculations for this indicator based a cohort of exiters who, other than possibly receiving follow-up services, have reached a four to six-month period of time since they were considered as an active WIOA participant. Usually, these individuals have not received a WIOA service for ninety days prior to their exit date. Thus, these individuals are often included in a "snapshot" measurement of employment for this indicator at a point in time when they may not have had any contact with a WIOA program staff person, or with a one-stop career center for seven to nine months.

In cases where unemployment insurance earnings records reveal that individuals are employed at the time the snapshot is taken, i.e.,

---

[58] Public Law 113-128, Section 116(b)(2)(A)(i)(I)

during the cohort period, their employment increases the numerator of employed exiters. However, not all employed individuals are included in unemployment insurance earnings records. Reporting supplemental data containing even a relative handful of participants, an employed individual could be the difference between passing or failing an indicator, or the difference between attaining a "B" or an "A." In order to capture the employed exiters who are not included in these records, and consequently not yet included in the numerator for the indicator, many local areas utilize a follow-up survey. Such a survey should include a cover letter, or embedded text, to remind the customer about their affiliation with the one-stop career center. The text should also briefly describe the purpose of the survey.

The survey itself should ask if the customer was employed during the crucial snapshot period that is required for that customer to be included in the denominator of the indicator. The dates of this period should be provided for the customer's reference. I have found that such a survey is usually most successfully conducted through a telephone call; however, because the majority of individuals who exit WIOA programs are indeed employed in the second quarter after exit, and also because the majority of the workforce is employed during daytime hours, chances are that the customer you are attempting to contact will be at work when you call. The response level might increase with supplemental forms of contact, such as calling after normal business hours, including snail mail with an easily returnable, yet confidential response card, email, text messages, apps, and online portals. While some local boards provide incentives for customers to respond, you should review these practices with the fiscal monitoring authority of your state oversight agencies before implementation.

Let me suggest something that is more important than means of contact or incentives, namely, the rapport you have established with the customer. As stated above, the snapshot taken of the customers contained in the cohort for this indicator might encounter them up to nine months after they participated in a WIOA activity. Beginning with an initial encounter with us, possibly including recruitment, intake, data element validation, assessment, career services (basic and individual), training services, supportive services, et al, a customer's association with the system might have lasted for a period of more than four years. Consequently, your request for supplemental data from the customer might come five years after you made a first impression. Therefore, it is important that the first impression be positive and lasting, and that you build upon and consistently reinforce that positive impression as much as possible with every succeeding interaction.

The need to establish, to maintain and to enhance a positive rapport with the customer takes us back to a foundational characteristic of a workforce professional, including passion, enthusiasm and providing customer satisfaction with products that melt. We must also understand that our record was compiled, not only with numbers, but with people. The degree of willingness for people to respond to our request for information is a measure of not only of how well we performed, but also of whether during our performance we also did what is right and what is good. The true workforce professional keeps their head and their heart in the right place, helping people, in a friendly professional manner.

Indicator:

"(II) The percentage of participants, who are in unsubsidized employment during the fourth quarter after exit from the program;"[59]

Suggestion:

The suggestion for this indicator is essentially the same as the previous one, with the exception of adjusting the cohort period to the fourth quarter after exit.

"Indicator:

(III) Median earnings of participants, who are in unsubsidized employment during the second quarter after exit from the program;"[60]

Suggestions:

---

[59] Public Law 113-128, Section 116(b)(2)(A)(i)(II)
[60] Public Law 113-128, Section 116(b)(2)(A)(i)(III)

The suggestion for this indicator is essentially the same as the previous two, with the exception of including an earnings question in the survey.

Indicator:

"(IV) The percentage of participants who obtained a recognized postsecondary credential or a secondary school diploma, or its recognized equivalent during participation in or within 1 year after exit from the program. A participant who has obtained a secondary school diploma or its recognized equivalent is only included in this measure if the participant is also employed or is enrolled in an education or training program leading to a recognized postsecondary credential within 1 year from program exit;"[61]

Suggestions:

As is the case with the above indicators, the survey can be used to capture information. In addition, local boards should establish a procurement process for training providers beyond their qualification for the state Eligible Training Provider List. While qualifying for the state list is a suggested element of the local board's procurement process, additional elements contained in a local request for proposals (RFP), such as timely reporting of the outcomes required for this indicator. In addition, the local board should design a reporting process through which training providers submit this data on a regular basis. Those RFP elements easily transfer into contractual obligations. Finally, whether career center staff chooses to use a case management approach or a less intensive customer management system, there must be an efficient, timely mechanism to capture the data required by this indicator before and after exit.

Indicator:

"(V) The percentage of participants who during a program year, are in an education or training program that leads to a recognized post-secondary credential or employment and who are achieving

---

[61] Public Law 113-128, Section 116(b)(2)(A)(i)(IV)

measurable skill gains, defined as documented academic, technical, occupational or other forms of progress, towards such a credential or employment."[62]

Suggestions:
The suggestions for this indicator are the same as the previous one.

Indicator:

"(VI) Effectiveness in serving employers, based on indicators developed as required by Section 116(b)(2)(A)(iv) of WIOA."[63]

The Final Rule for this indicator provides the following summary:

"The Workforce Innovation and Opportunity Act (WIOA) establishes six primary indicators of performance and defines five of those performance indicators. With this final rule, the U.S. Departments of Labor and Education (Departments) define the sixth performance indicator—effectiveness in serving employers—as Retention with the Same Employer and require it be reported by one WIOA core program on behalf of all six WIOA core programs within each State. This final rule incorporates two changes from the notice of proposed rulemaking (NPRM): the final rule does not limit the type of wage information that must be used, thereby permitting the use of supplemental wage information in the definition of the effectiveness in serving employers performance indicator, and it specifies that the definition is measuring retention in unsubsidized employment."[64]

Suggestions:

Both a participant-centered and an employer-centered approach are recommended to maximize results for this indicator. The participant-centered approach should replicate that which is suggested above under *"the percentage of program participants who are in unsubsidized employment during the second quarter after exit from*

---

[62] Public Law 113-128, Section 116(b)(2)(A)(i)(V)
[63] Public Law 113-128, Section 116(b)(2)(A)(i)(VI)
[64] Federal Register :: Workforce Innovation and Opportunity Act Effectiveness in Serving Employers Performance Indicator

the program." The employer-centered approach consists of conducting surveys of employers who are known to have hired program participants to confirm retention. The latter process will provide supplemental data in cases where wage information is not available. The survey process will also establish a customer feedback mechanism to enhance the relationship between the workforce development program and the employer.

For the youth program under Title I of WIOA, the indicators are:

<u>*Indicators*</u>:

"(I) Percentage of participants who are in education or training activities, or in unsubsidized employment, during the second quarter after exit from the program;

(II) Percentage of participants in education or training activities, or in unsubsidized employment, during the fourth quarter after exit from the program;

(III) Median earnings of participants who are in unsubsidized employment during the second quarter after exit from the program;

(IV) The percentage of participants who obtained a recognized postsecondary credential or a secondary school diploma, or its recognized equivalent, during participation or up to 1 year after exit. A participant who has obtained a secondary school diploma or its recognized equivalent is only included in this measure if the participant is also employed or is enrolled in an education or training program leading to a recognized postsecondary credential within 1 year from program exit;

(V) The percentage of participants who during a program year, are in an education or training program that leads to a recognized post-secondary credential or employment and who are achieving measurable skill gains, defined as documented academic, technical, occupational or other forms of progress towards such a credential or employment;

(VI) Effectiveness in serving employers, based on indicators developed as required by Section 116(b)(2)(iv) of WIOA."[65]

---

[65] Public Law 113-128, Section 116(b)(2)(A)(ii)(I)(II)(III)(IV)(V)(VI)

Suggestions:

The suggestions for youth indicators are essentially the same as those provided for the adults and dislocated workers indicators above, with two exceptions. One is that the methods of communication and the graphical design of contact material should be tailored to fit the youth audience. The second is that the service protocols for serving youth must include additional wrap around services and conformance with WIOA Youth Program requirements. Both topics are addressed in the chapter entitled "Youth Services."

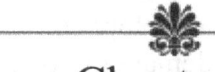

Chapter X
Return-On-Investment

The creative process is both misleading and mysterious, insofar as it can often seem to burst into our consciousness like a shooting star, only to fade into the night sky as quickly as it appeared. Why begin a chapter entitled "Return-on-Investment" by discussing creativity? The reason is that acts of creation, as well as the realization of what we have created, are the main events in the life of a workforce development system. Many have referred to the intimidating force of the "blank page" to a writer, and rightfully so, but the creative writer is more than someone trying to fill the blank page with words. The creative writer is a human being daring to accomplish something. In this context, those who enter into the wilderness of the blank page, putting pen to paper or fingers to keyboards, or who lend voices to recording devices, are brethren to explorers who embark upon a journey across a vast expanse of unknown territory, be it an ocean, the heavens, or uncharted lands. These intrepid adventurers are inspired, in my view by the divine, or at the very least by a higher power to which they respond by taking that most difficult step of all, the first one.

While creative writers might not necessarily be designated as writers according to their occupation, avocation or hobby, creative writing is an essential skill in many fields of endeavor, including that of the workforce development professional. Indeed, we must imagine, plan, propose and report to realize our vision for a workforce development system. State and local workforce development boards and their predecessors, for more than half a century, and perhaps longer, have been required to submit a plan in order to receive federal funding to operate a workforce development system. Grant applications require a proposed scope of work. Both of these documents require corresponding budgets and budget narratives.

Although these documents contain guidelines and specific interrogatory passages, omnipresent are the blank spaces that challenge aspiring workforce development system builders. For those tempted to walk the less demanding path, seemingly the best, or perhaps the most instinctive approach might be to avoid creating an imaginative plan or innovative grant application, and to instead offer only what is minimally required. With this minimalist philosophy, not only the actual writer(s), but the planners, the "imaginers," if you will, will likely get a "return" from of their minimal investment of effort, in the same measure of what they put into it, the minimum. In the context of the workforce development system, "the minimum" means less funding, less value to the community, lower performance, and an existential threat to the survival of the workforce development system and its boards of directors.

The creative process can seem deceptively simple because at the moment of illumination, a unique and original idea seems to reveal itself so easily. This is why a great songwriter might explain that a hit song was written in fifteen minutes. However, what that artist might not have explained is that the period of fifteen minutes during which the song was "written" was perhaps preceded by a period of writer's block. Furthermore, during the writer's block period, several textual or musical phrases that popped into the artist's head sounded like earth shattering original ideas, until the realization came that those ideas were actually the work of someone else. The point is that there is a period of incubation of an undetermined length, when ideas rise and fall like a tide, leading up to the "aha" moment when the song was effectively downloaded by the brain in fifteen minutes. And following that magical quarter hour there was doubtlessly another rather extended period of refinement before the finished product, the hit song was fully recorded, mastered and produced. When considering the amount of creative effort involved in imagining or re-imagining a workforce development system, or even a component project thereof, particularly beyond the bare minimum, a substantial amount of time, talent and grunt work is invested.

Talent is invested by people like you who are reading this book and who accept the premise that workforce development professionals not only have an obligation to their constituencies to be passionate and enthusiastic about their work, which in the planning stages might be described as dreaming a realistic dream, but who also will ultimately achieve a much higher level of self-realization and fulfillment by pursuing the maximum positive effect, instead of the minimum. After investing the forces of creativity into the design phase of workforce development programs comes the task of implementation, adjustment, evaluation and readjustment, i.e., execution. The execution phase figuratively moves more chips into the "pot" of the proverbial poker table. At this point, more staff, equipment, office space and other resources must be deployed. Partnerships that were developed during the planning phase, or that existed previously, must now be accelerated at full throttle. The support of board members, subcommittee members, service and training providers and businesses must be leveraged. Engaging our partners and other constituencies requires the investment of a priceless commodity, "trust." The value of this commodity is built over time through painstaking effort and consistent actions. And yet, the long and arduous process of building trust can be swept away like a beach house in a hurricane, instantaneously, with a single misstep.

Thus, the precious commodities of creative talent, time, hard work, and trusted relationships are all investments placed into our workforce development system. Note that while those commodities manifest an investment value almost beyond measure, we have not yet even included the value of taxpayer dollars. Those dollars are of course intrinsically connected to the other commodities mentioned. They are mentioned last here because dollars measure monetary price, but when that price is linked to the other commodities invested, the true value of the investment is more clearly revealed. Understanding the value of our investment leads us to appreciate the importance of realizing a return, both in monetary terms, and in terms that are more profound from a human perspective.

In view of the importance of evaluating and sharing the return on everything invested into workforce development programs, workforce development boards should develop a formula for a return-on-investment report. Such a report might be more of a work of art than science, as it is grounded in the study of economics, which arguably shares the same distinction. The report should be prepared in an attractive marketing format and distributed widely in hard copy and in an electronic format. In the best-case scenario, I believe it should be released in tandem with an annual report which, might also include data such as actual outcomes versus performance indicators, number of customers served, customer satisfaction outcomes versus goals, and other metrics ideally organized according the Malcolm Baldrige criteria for quality management.

The monetary portion of return-on-investment formula might include factors such as the formula funding allocation under various WIOA funding streams, including Adult, Dislocated Worker, and Youth. Entered employment rates may be used to project employment over a selected time period, preferably several years, to measure gains in tax dollars returned to the economy by newly employed workers and savings in welfare and unemployment insurance benefits costs. Beyond the mathematical formula, the report should demonstrate the return in human terms, as well.

As stated above, the return-on-investment report should be distributed in tandem with an annual report, which like the return-on-investment report is an excellent opportunity to market the value of the workforce development system to a variety of target audiences, including government officials, funders, businesses, partners, job seekers, to name a few.

In my opinion, the annual report should describe accomplishments that align with public priorities in a timely and thematic sense, while presenting statistical achievements and outcomes, performance indicators, opportunities for collaboration, testimonials, success stories, etc. Before composing these reports, the workforce development professional must ensure that they will be consistent with the WIOA requirements for the workforce development system infrastructure. This means that the reports must adhere to the required relationships between the local workforce development board, the local grant recipient and or sub-recipient(s), the fiscal agent, the one-stop operator, programs, partners and contractors.

With this understanding in mind, you must decide who is submitting the report to whom and about whom. For example, is the board submitting the report to the public? Or, is the one-stop operator submitting the report to the Board, which will subsequently share it with the public? This report should not conflate the functions of the board and the operator. It should be made widely available to the public as described under WIOA Section 134(c)(2)(A)(viii), as stated below:

viii) provision of information, in formats that are usable by and understandable to one-stop center customers, regarding how the local area is performing on the local performance accountability measures described in section 116(c) and any additional performance information with respect to the one-stop delivery system in the local area;"[66]

This suggestion echoes that which was made in the Chapter VII. - Career Services, which stated:

"An ideal way to share this information is through well-presented collateral material and/or reports that market the attributes and importance of the system, while where possible, communicating about its successes and defined by valid metrics."

Creating and publicizing formulaic return-on-investment data to justify the continued funding of workforce development systems is important because traditional workforce development program operators no longer enjoy a monopoly. Tasks related to administration and program operations, and workforce development board staffing have all become competitive market services. Complacency among those who currently are employed in these roles could lead to their being replaced by competitors. As the funding process continues to evolve and change, the need for informing the public about how our systems provide a return-on-investment was never greater.

It is a healthy practice for workforce development professionals to evaluate both the content and perception of their systems by browsing the web sites of other systems in their regions, states, nationally and internationally. This browsing should include, but not be limited to those that are WIOA-funded. For those funded by WIOA, it is helpful to not only review collateral material, but also workforce development board and subcommittee minutes. The purpose of this browsing activity is to stimulate creative planning based upon knowledge of what works well in other areas. By refreshing your creative juices in this manner, you might just improve your chances to design systems that yield an increased return-on-investment. So, get some rest, get some exercise, relax, spend time with those you love, and then, put your brain to work

---

[66] Public Law 113-128, Section 134 (c)(2)(A)(viii)

with the passion and enthusiasm it needs to create a system that achieves a maximum return-on-investment.

Chapter XI
Moving beyond business services, or are your business services B.S.?

Acronyms in workforce development meetings are like weeds in a garden. They may be both plentiful and unwelcome. So much so that one board chair with whom I served created a ban on acronyms, requiring that the terms they abbreviated are fully stated. As cumbersome as this might seem, it worked rather well. In fact, after the tenure of that chairperson, I continued the practice during my presentations and explanations. I found that many board members and others who do not operate in the workforce development program world every day preferred a comprehensive description of terms to the prospect of being lost in a discussion. Feeling lost in a discussion can breed apathy, and ultimately, lack of participation among board members and stakeholders. Counteracting that reaction leads us back to maintaining passion and enthusiasm in the board room and in our dealings with businesses.

One acronym that is usually not applied to the function of "business services" is of course the abbreviation of both words into the letters "BS." Ironically, while there are many outstanding business services practices, some indeed, might be appropriately labeled BS. Functioning under that dubious acronym might be intentional or due to lack of passion, enthusiasm and imagination. In any event, it is clear that in order to build and maintain the workforce development systems that our constituents deserve, outstanding business services are a key component and an essential foundation. One form of "BS" business services includes job development that merely replicates what is obviously available without third-party intervention, such as in cases where a job bank consists primarily of opportunities that the average individual is well-aware of through widely viewed help wanted signs, on-line listings and job boards, and newspaper postings. This negative practice is compounded when the openings include the least desired occupations, such as fast-food servers.

In my opinion, some employers who either send a general notice of employment availability or actual job postings to a career center, do not sincerely intend on hiring anyone through the office, but are attempting demonstrate compliance with real or perceived legal requirements. While there is no harm in erring on the side of providing information from the most easily discoverable sources, a problem would occur if a business services team, liaison, job developer or career counselor considers these actions to completely fulfill their responsibilities. This perception falls short of the vision that a workforce professional should aspire to.

Hailing from the age of the dinosaur, I remember when job orders existed in hard copy only. They were usually kept in binders. Whether maintained centrally or individually, there was usually some official version of the job bank to be shared by an entire job development team or unit. Not unlike a competitive sales or real estate office, some staff hoarded their individual favorites. While a team-oriented approach is preferred, the existence of individual competition in the delivery of business services can be an indicator of positive attributes. Using the analogy of a basketball team, as long as everyone on the team prioritizes the team winning before their own individual accomplishments, and as long as their court behavior is unselfish to the degree that they dish the ball to an open team mate, rather than force an individual shot, there is nothing wrong with wanting to excel individually. While I do not endorse individual hoarding of job leads, the tendency to compete internally does indicate the passion, enthusiasm, and competitive spirit that are essential for success. Succeeding in marketing anything requires a personality capable of being aggressive and assertive. It is therefore the role of the leadership to strike the right balance between internal competition and teamwork. Leaders must also foster individual and collective creativity among business services staff.

Perhaps some who are assigned to perform business services functions truly lack the traits necessary to penetrate the labor market on behalf of job seekers. Others might lack the proper motivation. Those in the latter category might be described, either appropriately or inappropriately as being lazy, or put more politely, unmotivated. In any event, leadership must play the critical role of getting excellent results from staff through motivation.

A mistake that leaders might make would be to assign a staff person to perform business services and then to lament that they are "not busy." But is that what you want for them to be? *Busy?* Or even less relevant, to *look* busy? Business services functions entail so much more than job development, marketing, or sales; however, even those elements of the operation do require some free space for staff to operate within. When staff assigned to perform business services functions do not appear to be busy, a misguided solution would be to give them a different and unrelated task, such as clerical or administrative work. This is usually a mistake because human nature often drives us to take the path of least resistance. For this reason, a staffer given different and completely unrelated duties will often prioritize the more routine and perhaps easier task.

If at the end of some measurement period, be it a day, or a week, or more, the staff person knows that they must show a work product for the most measurable task, i.e., number of files reviewed, or number of forms completed, as opposed to jobs or relationships developed. Thus, they are being motivated to prioritize what essentially began as busy work, rather than the more challenging task of job development. To be a job developer is challenging because developing jobs is relatively intangible and difficult to quantify in terms of time and efficiency, as well as any number of variables, including recalcitrant employers, the health of the labor market, the season, bad luck, etc.

This does not mean that job development activities cannot or should not be measured and evaluated for accountability and continuous improvement, but it does mean that dividing a worker's time due to lack of progress is often counterproductive. If the worker is giving you zero and you divide zero by two, you still end up with zero. Moving Beyond Business Services requires full engagement of the critical managerial and operational elements of leadership, teamwork, imagination, creativity, performance excellence and continuous improvement. All of those elements require…you guessed it, passion and enthusiasm, but that passion and enthusiasm must begin with business services leaders.

Who are the business services leaders? They are businesses, employers, workforce development board members, directors and staff, as well career center managers and supervisors. A common, and I believe, correct assertion among workforce development professionals is that the business customer is the primary customer that we serve. This is because without businesses, for the most part, including not-for-profit organizations, there are few jobs to develop or careers to prepare job seekers to enter and advance in. In terms of businesses, big dreams can benefit from big friends. This is not to say that willing business representatives of all sizes should not be welcome, but a single large employer can establish a credibility to the convening and brokering initiative that will enhance its brand and attract others. Workforce development leaders should not only target large employers from growing and emerging sectors doing business within their regions, but also and in particular, influential businesses that have actively volunteered to partner with the workforce development system.

Business-led business services can sometimes function without engaging WIOA-funded workforce development boards and they may also marshal a broader array of resources and a wider circumference of collaboration than is available from the WIOA-system alone. Such endeavors might not only be constructed for greater impact, but they also have the potential to create a relatively higher standard of comparison for workforce boards and their career centers. Private workforce development initiatives are often altruistic endeavors that augment the efforts of workforce development professionals working in publicly-funded programs. However, those same professionals must recognize the dangers of complacency in the scope of their vision, the depth of their ambition and the quality of their performance. On several occasions, colleagues have told me, "This program will be here forever because the nation needs it." In this context, those colleagues were referring to the subset of federally-funded and locally administered programs. My response to those colleagues was that while it is likely that some form of national workforce development system might continue within some level of perpetuity, it might not be operated by the current board, one-stop, contractor, or system we are working for, but rather by another more far-reaching and effective replacement.

All of the advocacy efforts of the publicly-funded system and all of the lobbying to raise legislative awareness about the need for workforce development systems will backfire on publicly-funded workforce professionals if they do not match their pleas with performance. That performance is not limited to surpassing negotiated performance indicator outcomes, but also includes effectiveness in continually establishing and asserting relevance to the economy and partners in the private sector, who could either be collaborators or competitors, depending upon how well they are engaged, or if they are engaged at all.

Workforce development partnerships with businesses will either never become airborne or be doomed to crashing and burning if the predicate for those partnership is, in the eyes of the workforce professionals, only that employer should be obligated to hire their job seekers. Hiring job seekers who have not been properly prepared and supported before hiring, and after, is a disservice to everyone involved, including the job seekers. This reality can place the publicly-funded workforce development system again in a position of competition, in this instance with other, differently funded programs. Employers need workers who not only are prepared with the academic and technical skills to do the work, but also those who are socially, psychologically and emotionally ready, as well. With this in mind, WIOA-funded boards must evaluate how well they might compete with other workforce development system models.

Just as WIOA-funded boards will benefit from identifying and partnering with private, business-led workforce development initiatives, so too, boards should, where feasible, curate partnerships with initiatives that were developed outside of the WIOA system, or what we might call "non-WIOA-initiatives" that either already engage employers at a significant level, or who, in concert with the board, could be leveraged to supercharge their partnerships. One anticipated objection to this suggestion is that "we," i.e., the board's one-stop system, does not have the staff to "compete" with a non-WIOA initiative. Well, that's fine because the local WIOA-funded system could be augmented by such an approach. On the other hand, if a partnership is not possible and the local WIOA-funded system wishes to go solo, the board should examine its expenditures to determine if it has fully invested its resources in approaches that are as sophisticated and cost effective as those developed outside of the WIOA system. From this same financial perspective, boards should consider contracting, either as a funder, or as a grantee, with privately operated initiatives which offer greater synergistic potential to both the WIOA-funded system and the larger system that might surround it. Forward and broad thinking boards will understand that the larger workforce development system is a universe that is constantly expanding and that the WIOA-funded system can either grow with it, or be dwarfed by it.

There might be those who will tell aspiring workforce development professionals that the organization that they work for cannot partner with potential competitors, even other workforce development boards because they might steal their methods, or their customers, or both. To me, this thinking is short-sighted and fainthearted. The better mousetrap invented today might be obsolete tomorrow. In modern times, we live in glass houses, but just as our ideas are shared through transparency, so too, transparency helps us to learn and evolve. You can be progressive and visionary, but still pragmatic.

I was fortunate to experience several partnerships with consequential workforce oriented large businesses. Having identified who business services leaders are and being cognizant of the importance of properly serving the business customer, the task before the workforce development professional is to engage the key business services leaders in planning, development and implementation activities. Those activities should begin with a big dream, a vision of what should and can be accomplished to achieve the highest quality of collective outcomes. Despite the need to collaborate with big friends, workforce development professionals should never relinquish their specific, statutory roles as partners to those friends. When a proper structure for interaction has been established and when mutual trust is demonstrated and maintained, then all of the "friends," i.e., partners, can dream big dreams together.

Speaking of dreams and dreaming, during my time a career counselor, I favored beginning a job development interview with a job seeker by asking what their dream job or career might be. Next, I would say that while I might not be able to help to completely fulfill that dream, knowing their goal, we would set off on a quest together and no matter how unlikely a destination of success might be, at the very least, we would be closer to the desired "dream destination" than when we started, and hopefully, eventually coming as close to achieving it as possible. The same approach applies to business services.

To move Beyond Business Services, our gaze must extend above and beyond job postings, referrals, interviews, salary negotiations, hiring and job fairs. All of those topics are important and relevant, but they exist under the larger and further reaching umbrella of a vision that is focused on our economy, quality of life and society. This is the time to think big. If you are the person that will be driving the conceptualization process, it might be best to mediate on the idea in a solitary manner before involving others in a collective brainstorming process. However, if your personality type thrives on the mental stimulation of working with a group, by all means take that route.

For the purpose of this discussion, let us imagine you are beginning in solitary fashion. With that in mind, a good starting point is to read the pertinent sections of the WIOA statute. As you read, or reread, as might be the case, maintain an internal perspective of viewing the world, the nation, your local workforce development area and your local workforce development system from a bird's eye view. WIOA requires regions and local workforce development areas to submit a new plan every four years, along with modifications to those plans during the intervening years. If you as a board director, or board staff person are leading the planning process, the concept you create for business services must be part of that plan. This is your opportunity to conceptualize business services from that bird's eye view to the extent that they are limited only by your imagination and the imaginations of others who eventually join the conceptualization process. Below is a discussion of how business services might be implemented in accordance with specific, required workforce development functions, which are indicated in bold.

Function: Convening

The above process guides you to plan in concert with businesses, which is a perfect opportunity to integrate a Beyond Business Services approach into the plan. Indeed...*The local board shall convene local workforce development system stakeholders to assist in...identifying non-Federal expertise and resources to leverage support for workforce development activities..."*[67]

Clearly, the activity of business services is one of those "workforce development activities" referenced above. For this reason, the plan

---

[67] Public Law 113-128, Section 107(d)(4)(B)(C)(D)

should describe a process whereby the businesses will be convened on a regular basis. Some progressive workforce development boards have industry sector standing committees. Whether convened by a standing committee, or through some other process, I feel that the convening should be organized around industry sectors that are statistical leaders in employment and growth in your regional economy.

An example of such a sector might be health care. Information technology might be another relevant sector, although it might look a little different from a traditional sector, in that it essentially cuts across a variety of sectors because of technical innovations that continually occur in the modern workplace.

Section 3(26) of WIOA defines industry sector partnerships as follows:

"The term "industry or sector partnership" means a workforce collaborative, convened by or acting in partnership with a State board or local board, that—

(A) organizes key stakeholders in an industry cluster into a working group that focuses on the shared goals and human resources needs of the industry cluster and that includes, at the appropriate stage of development of the partnership—

(i) representatives of multiple businesses or other employers in the industry cluster, including small and medium-sized employers when practicable;

(ii) 1 or more representatives of a recognized State labor organization or central labor council, or another labor representative, as appropriate; and

(iii) 1 or more representatives of an institution of higher education with, or another provider of, education or training programs that support the industry cluster; and

(B) may include representatives of—

(i) State or local government;

(ii) State or local economic development agencies;

(iii) State boards or local boards, as appropriate;

(iv) a State workforce agency or other entity providing employment services;

(v) other State or local agencies;

(vi) business or trade associations;

(vii) economic development organizations;

(viii) nonprofit organizations, community-based organizations, or intermediaries;
(ix) philanthropic organizations;
(x) industry associations; and
xi) other organizations, as determined to be necessary by the members comprising the industry or sector partnership."[68]

Sectors should be chosen based on sound scientific data and trusted anecdotal information. Federal, state and local labor market information should be studied and applied, along with pertinent articles and empirical evidence. While the employers that populate a sector might offer entry-level jobs, the sector should include occupations that open career pathways to workers who can progressively enhance their skills and credentials with education, training and stackable credentials. At a minimum, those career pathways should lead to middle skills jobs.

The process of convening businesses for sector partnership meetings should be expected to yield much more than compliance with the statute's description of the function of the board. I believe that it is important that the statute includes this function because that inclusion signals to me that what is already a valuable activity is also an "allowable" activity. The term allowable activity means that a local workforce development area is empowered to expend WIOA funds in its execution.

There are multiple reasons why convening businesses is a valuable activity. It provides an opportunity to enhance or create "relationships" with business leaders. It also creates a forum to engage businesses as partners, as opposed to as mere targets of marketing or job development solicitation. Relationships are the foundation of most business endeavors, and this one is no different. Like your friends and relatives at a barbecue, many, many employers do not understand what workforce development programs are really all about, much less who workforce development professionals are and what it is that they do. Using the prestige of the board to convene businesses, the behind-the-scenes technicians have an opportunity to meet, converse and bond with business leaders on a

---

[68] Public Law 128-113– Section 3(26)

professional and personal basis to achieve mutually beneficial objectives.

At these meetings, there is no need to overtly sell workforce development products, in fact, "selling" can interfere with, or even totally obfuscate the purpose for convening businesses. In one of my early forays into convening a business services meeting, I learned this lesson from a national workforce consultant. As the consultant and I were finalizing our presentation strategy on the morning of the meeting, before our guests arrived, he observed that I had provided meeting handouts containing brochures that emphasized financial reimbursements for on-the-job training and customized training, along with tax credit information. He stated that I was unwittingly establishing a Pavlov-like connection between myself, as a representative of the board, and money. While it is not wrong to inform businesses, at the appropriate point in time, of financial incentives available to them for appropriately participating in workforce development programs, with this subliminal, yet powerful, psychological link in place, it could potentially undermine a more important message.

The message is much larger and more consequential than a single hiring event. The message is that there is a big picture role that the workforce development plays in our economy, our society and our culture, and that role affects our quality of life. Without the proper orientation, some employers will see workforce development, including hiring and training employees, as a cost. To these employers, government funded financial incentives might seem as rightful offsets to those costs, which to a degree they are; however, workforce development is neither a cost, nor a financial incentive. It would only be perceived as such through a narrow and myopic lens. Workforce development is an investment. As such, it will cost the investors, some of whom are businesses, time and money; however, that investment should, when properly managed, yield dividends in terms of a skilled workforce that might represent a financial incentive beyond a one-time reimbursement or tax credit. The challenge of establishing workforce development as an investment conceptually is directly related to our earlier discussion of the perception in general, and specifically, among employers, of what workforce development is and who workforce development professionals are.

If I did not prioritize the message that workforce development is an investment in my meeting presentation and collateral material, how could it ever even register, let alone be prioritized in the minds of business representatives? Thus, workforce development professionals are tasked with ensuring that their business partners collaborate with them, not because they will be paid to do so, but because workforce development programs are essential to our mutual success, prosperity and survival. Even if solicitation of jobs or participation in training programs does occur, both businesses and workforce staff should understand that such activities are premature until a continuous cycle of shared learning is established. Partners from business, workforce development and other stakeholder groups must be like sponges, absorbing information and learning about each other's needs, problems, accomplishments, goals for the future, and more.

The reason many people do not understand what workforce development professionals do is probably that most people are not very familiar with a host of occupations that exist in the labor market. As workforce development professionals, it should not be a source of pride to be counted in that number. When we hear of a new company, indeed when we drive past a large office building, even when we consider an existing organization, or when we contemplate what we think we know about an occupation, or when we imagine how a traditional occupation might have been modernized, our passion and enthusiasm should translate into curiosity. As much as possible, we should speak the language of the business and they should speak ours. Our interaction with businesses should not be limited to a human resources or personnel department. This recommendation is not meant to disrespect human resources professionals, but rather to ensure that we attempt to engage decision-makers at the highest level. And when we meet those decision-makers, we should be ready.

Being ready includes providing a clear and concise description of how WIOA relates to the meeting we have convened, as well as supporting our verbal presentation with effective electronic and hard copy collateral material. A sector partnership meeting should be convened at an appropriate venue, such as within the workforce development board room, at a business headquarters, at a partner's facility, a college, economic development partner's office, or another appropriate location. The verbal presentation should be targeted and easily adapted to the audience.

Function: Brokering

A basic tenet of emergency management is that in an emergency a traditional chain of command may be temporarily suspended to establish a functional management structure that is the most responsive to the problem at hand. Under this type of scenario, egos are truly checked at the door and the team members focus on mission above status, credit and other distractions. A similar phenomenon takes shape when workforce development professionals engage in brokering. Once we establish a regular schedule for convening business services leaders, we can leverage the resources of this captive audience to create outstanding and imaginative workforce development programs.

With this prospect in mind, we must convene, not only business leaders as kind of the "stars" of our program, but also, a strong supporting cast. Not only are sector-based groups encouraged, but so too are thematic meetings that focus on particular initiatives. When the team is established, its founders should clarify who are team members and who are potentially and periodically invited guests. Drawing these distinctions will result in more focused and manageable teams.

Examples of supporting cast members to include at appropriate times include the following organizations: chambers of commerce and other business associations, colleges and universities, especially community colleges, organized labor, community-based organizations, faith-based organizations, organizations that serve special populations, economic development agencies, organizations that serve youth and/or older workers, the local social services district, and many others. The workforce development board has the opportunity through the convening process to create dream teams. With those teams in place, a cooperative agreement might be brokered. The cooperative agreement is forged in the interest of establishing the working parts of a program.

The program will operate as an engine, requiring the right working parts, including the resources of the team members who are on the field and potentially those that might be accessed from a strong bench. Some organizations, or their representatives might play a starring role for the creation of specific programs, while others play bit parts, and yet others, who are valuable teammates for other games or sports, i.e., programs, might not be involved in the project at hand. With proper cultivation of brokered relationships, everyone understands that there are times when they might lead, or follow, or be on the sideline. Ideally, there exists an esprit de corps that allows for a variety of organizations to combine forces, held in orbit by the "gravity" of the workforce development board and, more specifically, the workforce professionals who support it.

Function: Leveraging

In my view, leveraging should not be limited to accessing funds, but might also, or instead, it could mean accessing talent, staff, services, and more. Leveraging might mean augmenting a non-workforce development-centric project with workforce development programs and services. Cooperative agreements and partnerships can be created or augmented to maximize available resources in a well-coordinated manner for the purpose of leveraging.

Function: Employer Engagement

This section directs boards to:
"...develop effective linkages (including the use of intermediaries) with employers in the region to support employer utilization of the local workforce development system and to support local workforce investment activities."[69]

An intermediary used to develop a business services program might be a business association, a consultant, an economic development organization or even another business. Intermediaries help to break the ice that sometimes forms to block the trust and camaraderie between private sector and government entities. They should exist as a neutral third party to ensure the fair pursuit of mutually beneficial goals through reasonable means. In my experience, operating with a neutral coordinator results in more cooperation among partners and

---

[69] Public Law 113-128, Section 107(d)(4)(B)

helps to access grant funds in cases where the board is not directly eligible. This section also encourages the establishment of sector partnerships as follows:

"to develop and implement proven or promising strategies for meeting the employment and skill needs of workers and employers (such as the establishment of industry and sector partnerships), that provide the skilled workforce needed by employers in the region, and that expand employment and career advancement opportunities for workforce development system participants in in-demand industry sectors or occupations."[70]

This section also requires boards to utilize these sector partnerships...

"to ensure that workforce investment activities meet the needs of employers and support economic growth in the region, by enhancing communication, coordination, and collaboration among employers, economic development entities, and service providers;"[71]

The captive audiences, robust partnerships and emergency management structure-building techniques established under sector partnerships might position the board to create the desired career pathways systems required in the same section in the following passage:

"The local board, with representatives of secondary and postsecondary education programs, shall lead efforts in the local area to develop and implement career pathways within the local area by aligning the employment, training, education, and supportive services that are needed by adults and youth, particularly individuals with barriers to employment." [72]

Career pathways are defined in the WIOA statute under Section 3(7) as follows:

"The term "career pathway" means a combination of rigorous and high-quality education, training, and other services that—
(A) aligns with the skill needs of industries in the economy of the State or regional economy involved;

---

[70] Public Law 113-128, Section 107(d)(4)(D)
[71] Public Law 113-128, Section 107(d)(4)(C)
[72] Public Law 113-128, Section 107(d)(4)(5)

(B) prepares an individual to be successful in any of a full range of secondary or postsecondary education options, including apprenticeships registered under the Act of August 16, 1937 (commonly known as the "National Apprenticeship Act"; 50 Stat. 664, chapter 663; 29 U.S.C. 50 et seq.) (referred to individually in this Act as an "apprenticeship", except in section 171);[73]

(C) includes counseling to support an individual in achieving the individual's education and career goals;

(D) includes, as appropriate, education offered concurrently with and in the same context as workforce preparation activities and training for a specific occupation or occupational cluster;

(E) organizes education, training, and other services to meet the particular needs of an individual in a manner that accelerates the educational and career advancement of the individual to the extent practicable;

(F) enables an individual to attain a secondary school diploma or its recognized equivalent, and at least 1 recognized postsecondary credential; and

(G) helps an individual enter or advance within a specific occupation or occupational cluster."[73]

In order to design the career pathways envisioned by the framers in the above passage, I believe that sector partnerships should include all of the resources necessary for career counselors and participants to create individual employment plans (IEPs) for adults and dislocated workers and individual service strategies (ISS) for youth akin to electric circuits, which cannot be broken because of the presence of any missing connection. In this way, the sometimes-disparate resources for the partners for education, training, work-based learning, and supportive services, may be organized in a logical, sequential and/or concurrent manner, as appropriate to each individual participant.

In my opinion, an effective tool for planning career pathways within specific industry sectors is the U.S. Department of Labor's Competency-Based Model Clearinghouse.[74] This web-based product is useful to a variety of users, from industry sector partnerships, to

---

[73] Public Law 113-128, Section 3(7)

[73] https:/www.careeronestop.org/competencymodel

career counselors, to participants. The Clearinghouse's web site describes the initiative as follows;

"As part of the Industry Competency Model Initiative the Employment and Training Administration (ETA) and industry partners collaborate to develop and maintain dynamic models of the foundation and technical competencies that are necessary in economically vital industries and sectors of the American economy. The goal of the effort is to promote an understanding of the skill sets and competencies that are essential to educate and train a globally competitive workforce. The models serve as a resource to inform discussions among industry leaders, educators, economic developers, and public workforce investment professionals as they collaborate to:

- *Identify specific employer skill needs*
- *Develop competency-based curricula and training models*
- *Develop industry-defined performance indicators, skill standards, and certifications*
- *Develop resources for career exploration and guidance."*[75]

Sections 134(d)(vii)(I)(II) and 134(ix)(I)(II)(aa)(bb) of WIOA reinforce the imperative for and the methods of moving beyond business services described in this chapter with the passages cited below:

"(vii) activities—

(I) to improve coordination between workforce investment activities and economic development activities carried out within the local area involved, and to promote entrepreneurial skills training and microenterprise services;

(II) to improve services and linkages between the local workforce investment system (including the local one-stop delivery system) and employers, including small employers, in the local area, through services described in this section..."[76]

---

[75] https://www.careeronestop.org/competencymodel/getstarted/eta-industry-competency-initiative.aspx

[76] Public Law 113-128, Section134(d)(vii)(I)(II)

"(ix) activities to provide business services and strategies that meet the workforce investment needs of area employers, as determined by the local board...which services—

(I) may be provided through effective business intermediaries working in conjunction with the local board, and may also be provided on a fee-for-service basis or through the leveraging of economic development, philanthropic, and other public and private resources in a manner determined appropriate by the local board; and

(II) may include—

(aa) developing and implementing industry sector strategies (including strategies involving industry partnerships, regional skills alliances, industry skill panels, and sectoral skills partnerships);

(bb) developing and delivering innovative workforce investment services and strategies for area employers, which may include career pathways, skills upgrading, skill standard development and certification for recognized postsecondary credential or other employer use, apprenticeship, and other effective initiatives for meeting the workforce investment needs of area employers and workers;"[77]

Once we understand the many strategies to move beyond business services, and after the appropriate sector-partnership planning and professional relationship-building processes are put in place, the next timely task is to plan specific programs. At this point, we encounter an important fork in the road. The metaphorical "fork," in this context, is to limit or to expand our vision of workforce development programs. In support of expanding this vision, consider how WIOA Section 134(d)(1)(A)(i)(ii), describes "permissible local employment and training activities" for adults and dislocated workers below:

"(i) customized screening and referral of qualified participants in training services described in subsection (c)(3) to employers;

(ii) customized employment-related services to employers, employer associations, or other such organizations on a fee-for-service basis..."[78]

I feel that the above citation provides justification to local workforce development professionals to work with their boards and partners to imagine, design and implement countless project ideas. The process of creating these projects can engage and energize unused or underutilized partnerships, resulting in new synergies, while

---

[77] Public Law 113-128, Section 134(d)(ix)(I)(II)(aa)(bb)
[78] Public Law 113-128, Section 134(d)(1)(A)(i)(ii)

leveraging additional resources. For example, consider the following passage:

"*(ii) customized employment-related services to employers, employer associations, or other such organizations on a fee-for-service basis;*"[79]

With this passage, the WIOA framers seem to move the workforce professional beyond garden variety business services. The local board may now be considered as a reservoir containing expert consultants that local employers can not only engage to perform "customized employment-related services,"[80] but also, that employers will pay a fee to for the performance of these services. Not only are fees a source of new revenue, but they are also confirmation of your professionalism and expertise, in other words, they are a sign of respect. In setting up fee-for-services programs, local boards should take care to comply with the Code of Federal Regulations.

Another potential project idea could be founded on the following passage from Section 134(d)(1)(A)(vi)(I)(II):

"*(vi) employment and training activities provided in coordination with—*

(I) child support enforcement activities of the State and local agencies carrying out part D of title IV of the Social Security Act (42 U.S.C. 651et seq.);

(II) child support services, and assistance, provided by State and local agencies carrying out part D of title IV of the Social Security Act (42U.S.C. 651 et seq.);"[81]

This citation establishes authorization under WIOA for a local board to create a project with its local social services district. Under such a project, a local board could create a system for the local one-stop career center to recruit participants from the district's public assistance rolls to participate in employment and training programs. While a formal partnership between a social services district and a local one-stop career center system might seem like a no-brainer to some, in certain areas a close articulation between these intuitively

---

[79] Public Law 113-128, Section 134(d)(1)(A)(ii)
[80] Ibid.
[81] Public Law 113-128, Section 134(d)(vi)(I)(II)

linked partners might not be established to a meaningful degree. Whatever the level of partnership might be, and particularly if it is not well-developed, by being acquainted with, understanding and working to implement the spirit of this passage, a workforce development professional is working to ensure that a large and possibly untapped population of people in need of services, i.e., welfare recipients, i.e., poor people, benefit from WIOA resources in an organized manner. In addition, a "power partnership" between WIOA and social services should lead to a larger pipeline of workers who are being prepared to enter career ladders in the local labor market.

Because of the size of this population, the impact of their availability will be consequential to local employers. Thus, as two large human services players combine and focus resources, there is a greater probability that employers will desire to collaborate in the planning and design of career ladder preparation programs, so as to ensure that the impact of these new entrants into the workforce is positive for their businesses. The longer-term result could be more business involvement on the workforce development system, an enhanced talent pipeline, more hiring and retention of WIOA participants, higher wages, a larger footprint of the workforce development system and more influence accruing to the local board in shaping the hiring, training and development of workers in the local labor market.

The synergy that could be created from this program out flanks a lack of knowledge or understanding of our system or even a negative impression of it that might exist among employers in the business community. Creating partnerships, designing programs, and developing a robust talent pipeline is the picture in the local economy that is worth a thousand words. It is also a great accomplishment for the dedicated workforce development professional to play a part in such a worthy endeavor. And just think, it all started with simply reading the law. Section 134(d) also includes another of several calls for boards to establish sector partnerships and again encourages the use of business intermediaries. Section 134(b)(1)(2) differentiates between which activities "must" be conducted versus those that are merely "permissible" by dividing these activities, as stated below, into item

(1), which begins with the word "shall," and item (2), which begins with the word "may."

"LOCAL EMPLOYMENT AND TRAINING ACTIVITIES.—Funds allocated to a local area for adults under paragraph (2)(A) or (3), as appropriate, of section 133(b), and funds allocated to a local area for dislocated workers under section 133(b)(2)(B)—

(1) shall be used to carry out employment and training activities described in subsection (c) for adults or dislocated workers, respectively; and

(2) may be used to carry out employment and training activities described in subsection (d) for adults or dislocated workers, respectively."[82]

While the activities described under Section 134(d) are "permissible," Section 134(c)(2)(A) describes "Career Services[83] that must be performed *"at a minimum."*[84] The latter activities are understandably the most ubiquitous among the Nation's career centers. They are the essence of the retail services that the centers provide and, as such, are foundational to the existence and relevance of the WIOA-funded workforce development systems throughout the nation. Given the importance of these activities, they will be easily discovered by the workforce development professional who aspires to excellence.

What might not be discovered, are the activities contained in the section that, in my opinion, might not be as ubiquitous as those that most boards and career centers conduct as they serve adults and dislocated workers. Examples of the more commonly conducted services are group and individual counseling, classroom-based skills, training, on-the-job training, etc. Nevertheless, despite being mandated, below are selected excerpts from Section 134(b) that are less commonly conducted. These, less commonly conducted activities might potentially be foundational, not only to enhanced services for adults and dislocated workers, but also to programming options that may be integrated into the continuum of sector-based strategies, new partnerships and other initiatives that would be

---

[82] Public Law 113-128, Section 134(b)(1)(2)
[83] Public Law 113-128, Section 134(b)
[84] Public Law 113-128, Section 134(c)(2)(A)

appropriately categorized under the moniker of "Beyond Business Services," as follows:

"(c) REQUIRED LOCAL EMPLOYMENT AND TRAINING ACTIVITIES.—

(1) IN GENERAL.—

(A) ALLOCATED FUNDS.—Funds allocated to a local area for adults under paragraph (2)(A) or (3), as appropriate, of section 133(b), and funds allocated to the local area for dislocated workers under section 133(b)(2)(B), shall be used...

(iv) to establish and develop relationships and networks with large and small employers and their intermediaries; and

(v) to develop, convene, or implement industry or sector partnerships."[85]

Not only do these excerpts reinforce the suggestions and encouragement of the WIOA framers related to sector partnerships, but positioned in this section, despite their lack of practical ubiquity, these activities seem to be, by virtue of the word "shall," mandated.

The following section is noteworthy in that requires local boards, through their one-stop delivery systems, to provide:

(II) appropriate recruitment and other business services on behalf of employers, including small employers, in the local area, which services may include services described in this subsection, such as providing information and referral to specialized business services not traditionally offered through the one-stop delivery system;[86]

Section 134(c)(1)(2)(A)(xii) requires a list of services *"if determined to be appropriate in order for an individual to obtain or retain employment,"*[87] including: *"(VII) internships and work experiences that are linked to careers."*[88] Program operators might perceive an escape clause from conducting internships and work experiences for adults and dislocated workers in the phrase *"if determined to be appropriate."*[89] While it goes without saying that any intervention that is applied in the service of our customers should only be used as

---

[85] Public Law 113-128, Section 134(c)(I)(A)(iv)(v)
[86] Public Law 113-128, Section134(c)(2)(A)(iv)(II)
[87] Public Law 113-128, Section 134 (c)(1)(2)(A)(xii)
[88] Public Law 113-128, Section 134 (c)(1)(2)(A)(xii)(VII)
[89] Public Law 113-128, Section 134 (c)(1)(2)(A)(xii)

appropriate, the true workforce development professional does not seek escape clauses to avoid work that would benefit customers and advance the local system. That kind of thinking leads to under utilization of the resources that might otherwise be available due to permissions granted through WIOA and, of course, the limits of our imagination. We should be vigilant to ensure that we do not fail to, either through lack of research, or lack of desire, discover the full extent of WIOA permissions, and also, not limit our imaginations by lack of passion and enthusiasm.

While work experiences and internships seem to be more commonly utilized for youth programs, we must ensure that they are not underutilized for adults and dislocated workers. The benefit of these activities to adults is similar to those that accrue to youth. The greater use in youth programs might be due in part to the belief among some that work experiences and internships serve as a bridge between a young person who has either never been employed, or has little experience in the field that they are pursuing, and the workplace. However, many adults and dislocated workers fit the latter category. The application of work experiences and internships is a valuable element in the continuum of career pathways.

Consider the participants enrolled in your local adult and dislocated worker programs at the present time. Are there hundreds, perhaps thousands who are unemployed? What percentage of those individuals are currently engaged in a WIOA or partner program-funded activity beyond job search only? Within the cohort of participants enrolled in activities beyond job search, what percentage either have been, are currently, or will be enrolled in classroom-based skills training? What percentage of the same cohort either have been, are currently, or will be enrolled in basic education? Whatever the percentages and ultimately the numbers of participants that are included in the above categories, how many of them are prime candidates to participate in work experiences and internships?

Clearly, job search, when conducted properly, should be like a full-time job. Nevertheless, sacrificing a portion of the time devoted to job search to engage in work experiences and internships will usually pay dividends, especially since the law requires that they be *"linked to careers."*[90] These activities should be properly positioned

---

[90] Public Law 113-128, Section 134 (c)(1)(2)(A)(xii)(VII)

within a career pathways continuum to yield maximum benefits for the participant, an employer and the system at large. Proper positioning might be concurrent with or sequentially programmed to follow classroom-based skills training, and/or basic education, and where appropriate preceding additional work-based training, such as on-the-job training. The benefit of this robust continuum to the participant is the acquisition of pertinent experience, enhancement of a resume and/or career portfolio and additional learning to support classroom lessons.

The benefit to an employer is the acquisition of an additional worker. Although in the short term that employer may be losing some productivity in orienting, acclimating and training the intern, in the long-term the worker may provide a productive return-on-investment. Additionally, the system is benefiting from the relationship built with the employer, whereby the board and the employer are collaborating in the construction and maintenance of a talent pipeline. This example is one of many scenarios where the workforce development professional, by understanding and being true to the law, enhances services, not only to jobseekers, but to employers, i.e., businesses and therefore moves "Beyond Business Services," and also, can answer an affirmative "no" to the question "are your business services B.S.?"

Chapter XII
Work-Based Training

"Work-based training" is used here as an umbrella term for a variety of WIOA-funded activities, which when properly utilized, move beyond business services. While the discussion of work-based training is for all practical purposes an extension of the previous chapter, its complexity and possibilities warrant a separate examination. Work-based training activities are included in the comprehensive list of WIOA training activities for adults and dislocated workers provided below:

"(i) occupational skills training, including training for nontraditional employment;

(ii) on-the-job training;

(iii) incumbent worker training in accordance with subsection (d)(4);

(iv) programs that combine workplace training with related instruction, which may include cooperative education programs;

(v) training programs operated by the private sector;

(vi) skill upgrading and retraining;

(vii) entrepreneurial training;

(viii) transitional jobs in accordance with subsection (d)(5);

(ix) job readiness training provided in combination with services described in any of clauses (i) through (viii);

(x) adult education and literacy activities, including activities of English language acquisition and integrated education and training programs, provided concurrently or in combination with services described in any of clauses (i) through (vii); and

(xi) customized training conducted with a commitment by an employer or group of employers to employ an individual upon successful completion of the training."[91]

---

[91] Public Law 113-128, Section 134(c)(3)(D)

The following are selected work-based training activities included in the citation, along with descriptions of how these activities also benefit participants, employers and the system:

On-the-Job Training

The WIOA framers took care in defining and explaining the guidelines for on-the-job training, or "OJT." WIOA Section 3(44) defines OJT as follows:

"The term "on-the-job training" means training by an employer that is provided to a paid participant while engaged in productive work in a job that—

(A) provides knowledge or skills essential to the full and adequate performance of the job;

(B) is made available through a program that provides reimbursement to the employer of up to 50 percent of the wage rate of the participant, except as provided in section 134(c)(3)(H), for the extraordinary costs of providing the training and additional supervision related to the training; and

(C) is limited in duration as appropriate to the occupation for which the participant is being trained, taking into account the content of the training, the prior work experience of the participant, and the service strategy of the participant, as appropriate."[92]

Experienced workforce development professionals will recognize the long and complicated history that might have helped to forge this definition, and they will understand how the framers' expectations for the implementation of OJT have evolved from previous employment and training legislation. To those not privy to this history, understanding where we have been over the years with OJT will help to clarify where we need to be now and in the future. To achieve this understanding for those who are unfamiliar, and perhaps to stir some evolutionary memories, what follows is an analysis of the definition.

---

[92] Public Law 113-128, Section 3(44)

"The term "on-the-job training" means training by an employer that is provided to a paid participant while engaged in productive work..."[93]

This part of the definition establishes that the participant is paid during the training. In addition to the word "paid," another key word is the use of "productive" to define work. I interpret this to mean that a no-show, or otherwise inactive or less than serious form of work is not permissible.

"(A) provides knowledge or skills essential to the full and adequate performance of the job;"[94]

Here the framers seem to be telling us that the participant is expected to be fully qualified at the end of the training to retain and to perform the job.

"(B) is made available through a program that provides reimbursement to the employer of up to 50 percent of the wage rate of the participant... for the extraordinary costs of providing the training and additional supervision related to the training;"[95]

Because the definition requires that the program provide *"reimbursement to the employer"*[96] consisting of a percentage of the participant's wage, it is clear that the participant must be hired by the employer as an employee in order to command said wage. We also learn from this citation that the purpose of the reimbursement, which is the foundation of properly conducted OJT, must be *"...for the extraordinary costs of providing the training and additional supervision related to the training."*[97] If the purpose of the reimbursement is not for that which is stated above, then expenditure of funds for the OJT is out of compliance with WIOA and subject to disallowance. Disallowed costs are an epic failure for a workforce development program and its administrators.

---

[93] Ibid.
[94] Ibid.
[95] Ibid.
[96] Ibid.
[97] Ibid.

The purpose of OJT programs is not to essentially buy a job for the participant. In the first place, the law is the law and it does not sanction the purchase of jobs. Additionally, we should not need to buy a job for any participant. Whatever "baggage" the participant brings to a job application, employers and workforce development professionals need to understand that all job applicants, indeed all people, carry what could be described as "baggage," and the participant should be evaluated equally. Also, and this highlights our previous discussions of moving beyond business services to the point that we develop professional relationships with businesses, because of the mutual respect expected as an outcome of those relationships, employers should not be hiring participants because of arm-twisting or flimflamming, but rather because they comprehend and believe in the importance of OJT as a form of preparing workers to perform the jobs that their business needs to survive and thrive.

All of the work of the workforce development board and the system that it oversees is geared toward fostering and maintaining the talent pipeline that businesses need in order to access their most important resource, the human resource. Furthermore, the board and the system do not exist in a vacuum. They would cease to exist without a productive partnership with the business community. Consequently, the employer who hires a participant under an OJT program is agreeing to shoulder part of the load of the board and the system in developing the workforce. Essential to that commitment is the understanding on the part of the employer that hiring fully qualified and experienced new employees does not warrant the transfer of taxpayer funds from the government to the employer, not to mention that such a transfer is not allowable under WIOA as per this very definition. At the same time, if the employer cannot find an appropriately experienced and qualified worker, then it goes with the territory of the human resources management function that training a new employee, which will eventually yield the many dividends of a productive worker, will cost the employer something in terms of the temporary lower productivity of the worker, and will to some degree drain the productivity of supervisory personnel.

"(C) is limited in duration as appropriate to the occupation for which the participant is being trained, taking into account the

content of the training, the prior work experience of the participant, and the service strategy of the participant, as appropriate."[98]

When constructing WIOA-funded OJT, it is important to understand that neither the *"content of the training,"*[99] or the participant exist in a vacuum. I believe that this is an important concept because on the opposite side of the spectrum of an unjustified OJT program there lies another extreme, namely, an overly conservative interpretation of how OJT should be conducted. For example, some would say that if a dislocated worker was formerly employed as bookkeeper, then an OJT program to train that participant to perform the occupation of a bookkeeper is unwarranted. Thankfully, the above portion of the definition includes the phrase *"taking into account the content of the training, the prior work experience of the participant, and the service strategy of the participant..."*[100] From my perspective, this phrase prompts us to ask whether or not the bookkeeper has the skills and experience to perform the available job. For example, did the bookkeeper perform a similar job using a computer and or up-to-date software?" If not, a prorated duration would make sense. Finally, the requirement cited above of *"taking into account... the service strategy of the participant"* provides program operators with a protocol to document the justification for the OJT, including its duration, in consideration of the WIOA requirements that are included in this definition. The requirements for reimbursement levels for OJT are included in WIOA Section 134(c)(3)(H).

WIOA Section 181(a)(1)(A) requires that participants who are hired through OJT programs must: *"be compensated at the same rates, including periodic increases, as trainees or employees who are similarly situated in similar occupations by the same employer and who have similar training, experience, and skills, and such rates shall be in accordance with applicable law, but in no event less than the higher of the rate specified in section 6(a)(1) of the Fair Labor Standards Act of 1938 (29 U.S.C. 206(a)(1)) or the applicable State or local minimum wage law."*[101]

---

[98] Ibid.
[99] Ibid.
[100] Ibid.
[101] Public Law 113-128, Section 181(a)(1)(A)

WIOA Section 181(b)(5) states that *"Individuals in on-the-job training or individuals employed in programs and activities under this title shall be provided benefits and working conditions at the same level and to the same extent as other trainees or employees working a similar length of time and doing the same type of work."*[102]

The above citations and others contained WIOA, some of which refer explicitly to "on-the-job training" and some which refer to "programs and activities under this title," which include OJT, confirm that OJT participants have the same rights as other employees. There are numerous WIOA statutory and regulatory requirements for OJT which must be reflected in board policies, program operator procedures and contracts between the local grant recipient and/or grant sub-recipient/fiscal agent and employers participating in OJT programs. Rather than view the legal requirements for OJT, and indeed WIOA in general, as oppressive hindrances, the workforce development professional should look at them as valuable guidelines that give form and structure to the space in which we apply our passion, enthusiasm and intelligence to imagine and create high-quality career pathways programs for our participants and initiatives that move beyond business services for employers.

Incumbent Worker Training

WIOA Section 134(c)(3)(D)(iii) permits the work-based activity of incumbent worker training *"in accordance with subsection (d)(4)"*[103] This section states the following:
"(4) INCUMBENT WORKER TRAINING PROGRAMS.—
(A) IN GENERAL.—
(i) STANDARD RESERVATION OF FUNDS.—The local board may reserve and use not more than 20 percent of the funds allocated to the local area involved under section 133(b) to pay for the Federal share of the cost of providing training through a training program for incumbent workers, carried out in accordance with this paragraph.

---

[102] Public Law 113,128, Section 181(b)(5)
[103] Public Law 113-128, Section 134(c)(3)(D)(iii)

(ii) DETERMINATION OF ELIGIBILITY.—For the purpose of determining the eligibility of an employer to receive funding under clause (i), the local board shall take into account factors consisting of—

(I) the characteristics of the participants in the program;

(II) the relationship of the training to the competitiveness of a participant and the employer; and

(III) such other factors as the local board may determine to be appropriate, which may include the number of employees participating in the training, the wage and benefit levels of those employees (at present and anticipated upon completion of the training), and the existence of other training and advancement opportunities provided by the employer.

(iii) STATEWIDE IMPACT.—The Governor or State board involved may make recommendations to the local board for providing incumbent worker training that has statewide impact.

(B) TRAINING ACTIVITIES.—The training program for incumbent workers carried out under this paragraph shall be carried out by the local board in conjunction with the employers or groups of employers of such workers (which may include employers in partnership with other entities for the purposes of delivering training) for the purpose of assisting such workers in obtaining the skills necessary to retain employment or avert layoffs.

(C) EMPLOYER PAYMENT OF NON-FEDERAL SHARE.—

Employers participating in the program carried out under this paragraph shall be required to pay for the non-Federal share of the cost of providing the training to incumbent workers of the employers.

(D) NON-FEDERAL SHARE.—

(i) FACTORS.—Subject to clause (ii), the local board shall establish the non-Federal share of such cost (taking into consideration such other factors as the number of employees participating in the training, the wage and benefit levels of the employees (at the beginning and anticipated upon completion of the training), the relationship of the training to the competitiveness of the employer and employees, and the availability of other employer-provided training and advancement opportunities.

(ii) LIMITS.—The non-Federal share shall not be less than—

(I) 10 percent of the cost, for employers with not more than 50 employees;

(II) 25 percent of the cost, for employers with more than 50 employees but not more than 100 employees; and

(III) 50 percent of the cost, for employers with more than 100 employees.

(iii) CALCULATION OF EMPLOYER SHARE.—The non-Federal share provided by an employer participating in the program may include the amount of the wages paid by the employer to a worker while the worker is attending a training program under this paragraph.

The employer may provide the share in cash or in kind, fairly evaluated."[104]

While the guidelines for incumbent worker training under WIOA are relatively straight forward, it is important for the workforce development professional to recognize that this section of the law echoes what I perceive as an overarching theme contained in guidance for WIOA-funded work-based training, namely that these programs are not meant to be operated in a vacuum. The guidance requires consideration of the *"characteristics of the participants,"*[105] *the relationship of the training to the competitiveness of a participant and the employer,"*[106] *and the wage and benefit levels of those employees (at present and anticipated upon completion of the training) ..."*[107]

Transitional Jobs in Accordance with Subsection (d)(5)

"Subsection (d)(5) is part of the WIOA Section 134(d) PERMISSIBLE LOCAL EMPLOYMENT AND TRAINING ACTIVITIES, which includes the statement below.

"The local board may use not more than 10 percent of the funds allocated to the local area involved under section 133(b) to provide transitional jobs under subsection (c)(3) that—

---

[104] Public Law 113-128, Section 134(d)(4)(A)(i)(ii)(I)(II)(III)(iii)(B)(C)(D)(i)(ii)(I)(II)(III)(iii)
[105] Ibid.
[106] Ibid.
[107] Ibid.

(A) are time-limited work experiences that are subsidized and are in the public, private, or nonprofit sectors for individuals with barriers to employment who are chronically unemployed or have an inconsistent work history;

(B) are combined with comprehensive employment and supportive services; and

(C) are designed to assist the individuals described in subparagraph (A) to establish a work history, demonstrate success in the workplace, and develop the skills that lead to entry into and retention in unsubsidized employment."[108]

As was the case with OJT, all of the activities described under WIOA Section 134(b)(3)(D), and particularly those discussed in this chapter, should be supported, either by overarching policies established by the local workforce development board, or by an individually specific policy. This clearly applies to the activity of transitional jobs because of the need to specifically define certain terms. For example, the term "time-limited" should be a specific number of work hours. The reason that hours must be used is that the hours in a day, month or year could vary. Furthermore, terms such as "barriers to employment," "chronically unemployed" and "inconsistent work history" should be universally defined by the local board to provide clear guidelines to career center staff who recruit, select and enroll participants in transitional jobs programs, so as to avoid inconsistency in the expenditure of WIOA funds.

The framers included the requirement that transitional jobs "*are combined with comprehensive employment and supportive services...*"[109] With this requirement, in a similar fashion to the manner in which detailed qualifying guidance was provided to ensure the quality of on-the-job training programs, the framers seem to be telling us that a transitional job should be more than a job and be an important wrung on the ladder of an individual employment plan or service strategy. To ensure that the participant does not fall off that ladder, to ensure that the wrung does not break, the workforce development system must support participants throughout their ascent with effective wrap-around services. This section of the law informs us further that the outcome of having participated in a

---

[108] Public Law 113-128, Section 134(d)(5)(A)(B)(C)
[109] Ibid.

transitional jobs program should be *"to assist the individuals ... to establish a work history, demonstrate success in the workplace, and develop the skills that lead to entry into and retention in unsubsidized employment."*[110] The statement *"that lead to entry into and retention in unsubsidized employment,"*[111] seems to further underscore the importance of utilizing transitional jobs programs for *"individuals with barriers to employment who are chronically unemployed or have an inconsistent work history."*[112]

While a local career center might successfully develop transitional jobs programs on an individual and as-needed basis, this is an activity that the sector-based partnerships, described earlier, might plan and execute on a large scale, involving multiple participants and employers, to achieve maximum positive impact for businesses, participants and the community. Through sector-based partnerships, businesses can identify the skills they need to acquire from a talent pipeline. Entry level workers can be recruited to enter career pathways that may be traversed through a variety of interventions, including transitional jobs. With the right non-business partners at the table, efficient, broad-based sources of recruitment may be established. Examples of such recruitment sources include the local social services district, the criminal justice system and Job Corps. The community might benefit from transitional jobs because community-based organizations, libraries, public agencies and non-profit organizations might act as work sites, in addition to private sector employers. With this larger vision in mind, the workforce development professional should view the opportunity to conduct a transitional jobs program not only as an activity to be selected, as appropriate, to assist a jobseeker, but as a component of a strategy that marshals the resources of business, one-stop partners and the workforce to achieve the larger goals of full employment and the establishment and maintenance of a skilled workforce, a booming economy and an improved quality of life for the community.

---

[110] Ibid.
[111] Ibid.
[112] Ibid.

Chapter XIII
Youth

Perhaps I am overly sentimental, but when I encounter a child, whether they be a sweet infant, or a dirty-faced dreamer on a sandlot on the first day of summer, it hits me in the gut to wonder about where they are coming from, where they are now, and where they are going. If you have ever seen a toddler, who loves you and whom you love back, come running to greet you, then you understand what it is like to be awash in pure love wrapped in a ribbon of innocence. It is sad to think that, although we retain elements of our childhood selves within our consciousness throughout our lives, the toddler that comes running up to us, is soon, in many respects, gone forever, at least in this lifetime.

Even at a tender age, one thing that surely unravels, frays and disappears, sometimes suddenly and even painfully, is innocence. In a bittersweet sense, children are unaware that they possess innocence, until they lose it. And once innocence is lost, sadly, it is gone, never to return. Although innocence can be permanently lost, faith, hope, love and wonder do not have to be. As children grow up, they can still dream of and achieve bright futures and they can maintain their enthusiasm, passion and imagination.

It seems doubtful that anyone who achieved a dream in life did so without people who helped them along the way. Workforce development professionals are entrusted to help the people that they serve to achieve their dreams, or at least to try. All of the people we serve, either were at one time, or technically still are children, so their dreams should never die, particularly on our watch.

Section 129 of WIOA describes the "USE OF FUNDS FOR YOUTH WORKFORCE INVESTMENT ACTIVITIES."[113] Section 129(c)(1) describes the "Program Design,"[114] which, in addition to

---

[113] Public Law 113-128, Section 129
[114] Public Law 113-128, Section 129(c)(1)

comprehensive assessment and the development of individual service strategies, must provide the following:

"*(i) activities leading to the attainment of a secondary school diploma or its recognized equivalent, or a recognized postsecondary credential;*

(ii) preparation for postsecondary educational and training opportunities;

(iii) strong linkages between academic instruction (based on State academic content and student academic achievement standards established under section 1111 of the Elementary and Secondary Education Act of 1965 (20 U.S.C. 6311)) and occupational education that lead to the attainment of recognized postsecondary credentials;

(iv) preparation for unsubsidized employment opportunities, in appropriate cases; and

(v) effective connections to employers, including small employers, in in-demand industry sectors and occupations of the local and regional labor markets; and..."[115]

The U.S. Department of Labor provided additional instructions which augment the requirements for the Youth Program Design in Training and Employment Guidance Letter (TEGL) Number 21-16. Included in the TEGL are explicit "assessment requirements."[116] The requirements include the following:"

"*The WIOA youth Program Design requires an objective assessment of academic levels, skill levels, and service needs of each participant, which includes a review of basic skills, occupational skills, prior work experience, employability, interests, aptitudes, supportive service needs, and developmental needs. Assessments must also consider a youth's strengths rather than just focusing on areas that need improvement. As discussed in 20 CFR § 681.290, "in assessing basic skills, local programs must use assessment instruments that are valid and appropriate for the target population, and must provide reasonable accommodation in the assessment process, if necessary, for individuals with disabilities." For purposes*

---

[115] Public Law 113-128, Section129 (c)(1)(C)(i)(ii)(iii)(iv)(v)

[116] Training and Employment Guidance Letter Number 21-16 Operating Guidance for Workforce Innovation and Opportunity Act, Employment and Training Advisory System, United States Department of Labor, March 2, 2017

of the basic skills assessment portion of the objective assessment, local programs are not required to use assessments approved for use in the Department of Education's National Reporting System (NRS), nor are they required to determine an individual's grade level equivalent or educational functioning level (EFL), although use of these tools is permitted. Rather, local programs may use other formalized testing instruments designed to measure skills-related gains. It is important that, in addition to being valid and reliable, any formalized testing used be appropriate, fair, cost effective, well-matched to the test administrator's qualifications, and easy to administer and interpret results. Alternatively, skills related gains may also be determined through less formal alternative assessment techniques such as observation, folder reviews, or interviews. The latter may be particularly appropriate for youth with disabilities given accessibility issues related to formalized instruments. Local programs may use previous basic skills assessment results if such previous assessments have been conducted within the past six months. In contrast to the initial assessment described above, if measuring EFL gains after program enrollment under the measurable skill gains indicator, local programs must use an NRS approved assessment for both the EFL pre- and post-test to determine an individual's educational functioning level."[117]

TEGL #21-16 also provides guidance on the use of incentives for youth with the following passage:

"20 CFR § 681.640 states that "incentive payments to youth participants are permitted for recognition and achievement directly tied to training activities and work experiences. The local program must have written policies and procedures in place governing the award of incentives and must ensure that such incentive payments are tied to the goals of the specific program; outlined in writing before the commencement of the program that may provide incentive payments; align with the local program's organizational policies; and are in accordance with the requirements contained in 2 CFR part 200." DOL included the reference to the Uniform Guidance at 2 CFR part 200 to emphasize that while incentive payments are allowable under WIOA, the incentives must be in compliance with

---

[117] Ibid.

the Cost Principles in 2 CFR part 200. For example, Federal funds must not be spent on entertainment costs. Therefore, incentives must not include entertainment, such as movie or sporting event tickets or gift cards to movie theaters or other venues whose sole purpose is entertainment. Additionally, there are requirements related to internal controls to safeguard cash, which also apply to safeguarding of gift cards, which are essentially cash. While DOL recognizes that incentives could be used as motivators for various activities such as recruitment, submitting eligibility documentation, and participation in the program, incentives paid for with WIOA funds must be connected to recognition of achievement of milestones in the program tied to work experience, education, or training. Such incentives for achievement could include improvements marked by acquisition of a credential or other successful outcomes. Local areas may leverage private funds for incentives that WIOA cannot fund. Incentive payments may be provided to both ISY and OSY as long as they comply with the requirements of 20 CFR § 681.640."[118]

In addition to providing guidance regarding the youth Program Design, the TEGL also reinforces the necessity to create firewalls in the construction and operation of the overarching workforce development system with the following requirements:

"If Local WDBs decide to directly provide youth services, DOL recognizes that situations may arise where a single entity performs multiple roles, such as fiscal agent, service provider, or One-Stop operator. In such situations, 20 CFR § 679.430 requires "a written agreement with the Local WDB and Chief Elected Official (CEO) to clarify how the organization will carry out its responsibilities while demonstrating compliance with WIOA and corresponding regulations, relevant Office of Management and Budget circulars, and the State's conflict of interest policy."

Furthermore, separation of roles for staff to the Local WDB and the role of the fiscal agent described in 20 CFR §s 679.400 and 679.420, respectively, provide more clarity on the distinct functions of these entities. When youth services are provided by an entity that fulfills another role in the local area, the agreement with the Local WDB and CEO must provide clarity on the expectations for those

---

[118] Ibid.

roles and clear methods of tracking effective execution and accountability for the distinct roles."[119]

After describing the requirements for the Youth Program Design, WIOA describes the requirements for the "Program Elements"[120] at Section 129(c)(2), which states:

"In order to support the attainment of a secondary school diploma or its recognized equivalent, entry into postsecondary education, and career readiness for participants, the programs described in paragraph (1) shall provide elements consisting of—

(A) tutoring, study skills training, instruction, and evidence-based dropout prevention and recovery strategies that lead to completion of the requirements for a secondary school diploma or its recognized equivalent (including a recognized certificate of attendance or similar document for individuals with disabilities) or for a recognized postsecondary credential;

(B) alternative secondary school services, or dropout recovery services, as appropriate;

(C) paid and unpaid work experiences that have as a component academic and occupational education, which may include—

(i) summer employment opportunities and other employment opportunities available throughout the school year;

(ii) pre-apprenticeship programs;

(iii) internships and job shadowing; and

(iv) on-the-job training opportunities;

(D) occupational skill training, which shall include priority consideration for training programs that lead to recognized postsecondary credentials that are aligned with in demand industry sectors or occupations in the local area involved, if the local board determines that the programs meet the quality criteria described in section 123;

(E) education offered concurrently with and in the same context as workforce preparation activities and training for a specific occupation or occupational cluster;

---

[119] Ibid.
[120] Public Law 113-128, Section 129(c)(2)

(F) leadership development opportunities, which may include community service and peer-centered activities encouraging responsibility and other positive social and civic behaviors, as appropriate;

(G) supportive services;

(H) adult mentoring for the period of participation and a subsequent period, for a total of not less than 12 months;

(I) follow-up services for not less than 12 months after the completion of participation, as appropriate;

(J) comprehensive guidance and counseling, which may include drug and alcohol abuse counseling and referral, as appropriate;

(K) financial literacy education;

(L) entrepreneurial skills training;

(M) services that provide labor market and employment information about in-demand industry sectors or occupations available in the local area, such as career awareness, career counseling, and career exploration services; and

(N) activities that help youth prepare for and transition to postsecondary education and training."[121]

Allowable expenditures for work experience are addressed in TEGL # 21-16 with the following passage:

"TEGL No. 8-15 provides further discussion of allowable expenditures that may be counted toward the work experience expenditure requirement and articulates that program expenditures on the work experience program element can be more than just wages paid to youth in work experience. Allowable work experience expenditures include the following: • Wages/stipends paid for participation in a work experience; • Staff time working to identify and develop a work experience opportunity, including staff time spent working with employers to identify and develop the work experience; • Staff time working with employers to ensure a successful work experience, including staff time spent managing the work experience; • Staff time spent evaluating the work experience; • Participant work experience orientation sessions; • Employer work experience orientation sessions; • Classroom training or the required academic education component directly related to the work

---

[121] Public Law 113-128, Section 129(c)(2)(A)(B)(C)(D)(E)(F)(G)(H)(I)(K)(L)(M)(N)

experience; • Incentive payments directly tied to the completion of work experience; and • Employability skills/job readiness training to prepare youth for a work experience. Supportive services are a separate program element and cannot be counted toward the work experience expenditure requirement even if supportive services assist the youth in participating in the work experience."[122]

TEGL # 21-16 provides "Additional Notes and Reporting Program Elements"[123] with the following passage: *Documenting receipt of Program Elements is critical to ensure that youth who are actively participating in programs do not get unintentionally exited due to 90 days of no service. All 14 WIOA youth Program Elements are contained in the PIRL and local youth programs should ensure that services received are reported in the applicable program element in the PIRL. 23 In addition, note that case management is the act of connecting youth to appropriate services and not a program element. Case managers providing case management should not be reported as one of the 14 youth Program Elements in the PIRL."*[124]

Note: The acronym "PIRL" abbreviates the term Participant Individual Record Layout."[125]

One method the local boards might use to ensure that the data needed to document these services is collected at the earliest point possible would be to create a reporting form to be used by youth service providers. The form would be designed to include fields for each Program Element. To better understand the purposes of and relationship between the Program Design and the Program Elements, it might help to think of the Program Design as a destination and the Program Elements as the means of transportation to reach that destination. I view these two passages of the WIOA law as two legs on a three-legged stool needed to construct effective youth programs. The third leg is the definition of eligible youth, which is defined in

---

[122] Training and Employment Guidance Letter Number 21-16 Operating Guidance for Workforce Innovation and Opportunity Act, Employment and Training Advisory System, United States Department of Labor, March 2, 2017
[123] Ibid.
[124] Ibid.
[125] https://www.dol.gov/agencies/eta/performance/reporting

several passages. Section 3(18) states: *"the term eligible youth means in-school or out-of school youth."*[126]

Section 129(a)(1)(B) defines out-of-school youth as follows:
"...the term ''out-of-school youth'' means an individual who is—
    (i) not attending any school (as defined under State law);
    (ii) not younger than age 16 or older than age 24; and
    (iii) one or more of the following:
        (I) A school dropout.
        (II) A youth who is within the age of compulsory school attendance, but has not attended school for at least the most recent complete school year calendar quarter
        (III) A recipient of a secondary school diploma or its recognized equivalent who is a low-income individual and is (aa) basic skills deficient; or (bb) an English language learner.
        (IV) An individual who is subject to the juvenile or adult justice system.
        (V) A homeless individual (as defined in section 41403(6) of the Violence Against Women Act of 1994 (42 U.S.C. 14043e–2(6))), a homeless child or youth (as defined in section 725(2) of the McKinney-Vento Homeless Assistance Act (42 U.S.C. 11434a(2))), a runaway, in foster care or has aged out of the foster care system, a child eligible for assistance under section 477 of the Social Security Act (42 U.S.C. 677), or in an out-of-home placement.
        (VI) An individual who is pregnant or parenting.
        (VII) A youth who is an individual with a disability.
        (VIII) A low-income individual who requires additional assistance to enter or complete an educational program or to secure or hold employment."[127]

Section 129(a)(1)(C) describes in-school youth as follows:
"the term ''in-school youth'' means an individual who is—
    (i) attending school (as defined by State law);

---

[126] Public Law 113-128, Section 3(18)
[127] Public Law 113-128, Section 129(a)(1)(B)(i)(ii)(iii)(I)(II)(III)(I)(II)(III)(IV)(V)(VI)(VII)(VIII)

> (ii) not younger than age 14 or (unless an individual with a disability who is attending school under State law) older than age 21;
> (iii) a low-income individual; and
> (iv) one or more of the following:
> > (I) Basic skills deficient.
> > (II) An English language learner.
> > (III) An offender.
> > (IV) A homeless individual (as defined in section 41403(6) of the Violence Against Women Act of 1994 (42 U.S.C. 14043e–2(6))), a homeless child or youth (as defined in section 725(2) of the McKinney-Vento Homeless Assistance Act (42 U.S.C. 11434a(2))), a runaway, in foster care or has aged out of the foster care system, a child eligible for assistance under section 477 of the Social Security Act (42 U.S.C. 677), or in an out-of-home placement.
> > (V) Pregnant or parenting.
> > (VI) A youth who is an individual with a disability.
> > (VII) An individual who requires additional assistance to complete an educational program or to secure or hold employment."[128]

Obviously, these definitions are important to program operators who must select individuals to serve who meet eligibility criteria, but they carry a message of greater significance to a workforce development professional, regardless of their position, whether they are an intake counselor or a workforce board member. Each criterion signals to all categories of the organization, including the board and its youth program infrastructure, that robust partnerships must be developed and maintained.

For example, *"an individual who is subject to the juvenile or adult justice system,"*[129] indicates that the board should ensure the its program operators establish close working relationships with a

---

[128] Public Law 113-128, Section 129(a)(1)(C)(i)(ii)(iii)(iv)(I)(II)(III)(I)(II)(III)(IV)(V)(VI)(VII)
[129] Public Law 113-128, Section 129(a)(1)(B)(IV)

myriad of organizations involved with this segment of the youth population, from the correctional facilities to faith-based organizations. The same connections should exist with the local social services district to collaborate in serving *"A homeless individual...,"[130]* and so forth. The required partners under the WIOA statute, as well others that are not mandated, should also be included, as appropriate.

Successful WIOA youth programs are like a large boulder, that is immovable in the hands of a single or a few individuals, but that can soar to the sky when lifted by many. The work involved in creating, operating and maintaining these programs is one of the clearest examples of the distinction between someone who only toils in the field of workforce development and someone who has attained the status of a workforce development professional. Attainment of that status will offer you both personal and professional fulfillment. This is because yours are among the hands that almost miraculously lift that immovable boulder to the heights, signifying that you are changing the lives of our most vulnerable youth, and improving their ability to impact on that most essential foundation to our survival and prosperity, the future.

The antithesis of the workforce development professional philosophy would be to view the processes of operating youth programs as a stand-alone endeavor. Successful programs must begin with the kind of creative visioning process, including the planning and development described in our discussion of moving "beyond business services." And speaking, of moving beyond business services, the stakeholders that correspond to the youth eligibility criteria should be included in the board sector-based partnership initiatives. Furthermore, in view of the complexity and uniqueness of WIOA youth programs, appointment of a youth standing committee, established under the proper charter, is an important strategic planning action. Although youth subcommittees to the board were mandated under the Workforce Investment Act, establishment a youth standing committee seems to be optional under WIOA. The law states:

"(STANDING COMMITTEES.—

---

[130] Ibid.

(A) IN GENERAL.—The local board may designate and direct the activities of standing committees to provide information and to assist the local board in carrying out activities under this section. Such standing committees shall be chaired by a member of the local board, may include other members of the local board, and shall include other individuals appointed by the local board who are not members of the local board and who the local board determines have appropriate experience and expertise. At a minimum the local board may designate each of the following:...(ii) A standing committee to provide information and to assist with planning, operational, and other issues relating to the provision of services to youth, which shall include community-based organizations with a demonstrated record of success in serving eligible youth."[131]

Ideally, the youth standing committee should be constructed with the key stakeholder constituencies that correlate to the youth eligibility criteria. Constructed in this manner, the committee will naturally include representatives of the collaborating partners necessary to ensure full representation of youth target groups. Developing and maintaining these partner relationships should occur not only at committee meetings, but at sector-partnership events, and of course, during day-to-day operations. These relationships should be manifest in the development of individual service strategies, shared work-based learning activities, and shared job leads. Effective partnerships not only leverage funding more efficiently, but they maximize the synergy between other organizations, including businesses, resulting in a more powerful workforce development system and enhanced services for youth. The power of these partnerships, applied at every level of planning and development across multiple organizational constituencies, underscores the importance of operating something greater and more significant than youth "programs," something we might call "the workforce development system for youth."

Several times I have referred to a bird's eye view. This does not mean that workforce development leaders cannot see the forest for the trees. Indeed, the trick is for us to see from the point of view of an eagle, but to maintain the ability to swoop down to the ground and understand what happens there and everything in between. In a

---

[131] Public Law 113-128, Section 107(b)(4)(A)(ii)

philosophical sense, the chief elected official(s), the board, the youth standing committee, the grant sub-recipient, the fiscal agent, program operators, contractors, staff, businesses, partners, participants, parents, the general public, funders, etc., are all part of the same organism and the workforce development professional's "eyes" must be able to view the workforce development system from all of these perspectives.

Chapter XIV
The Great White Whale and Other Grants

As with other occupations in which people spend huge amounts of time in an office, behind a desk and in front of a computer, there have been many times in my career when I longed for a more adventurous existence. A coworker and kindred spirit of mine once described this feeling by explaining that at heart we were "cowboys." If not a cowboy, my wanderlust might have been equally fulfilled by being a sailor. I would have signed up for a new voyage in the open sea most days. In the field of workforce development, one of the most adventurous activities we might undertake is the pursuit of regional, future-changing grants. In my career, there have been several great white whale grant opportunities that I applied for, but never did capture. Of the many grants that I played a role in winning, some fell into my lap, some were moderately difficult to win, and some were of the future-changing nature. I found that in all cases it is of paramount importance, when applying for grants, to fully understand the grant instructions, to know who you are as an organization and to consider who will be reviewing your proposal.

In the workforce development industry innovation and simplicity seem to wrestle on a tightrope, while the grant writer must constantly ensure that neither falls, because there is no net below. This wrestling match is particularly relevant in the case of some of the larger, more challenging applications for which grant application reviewers are often not experts in the field of workforce development, while the application contains intricate questions that tempt the grant writer to describe complex "inside baseball" operations. While the text and arithmetic calculations must ideally be error free, and while the writing must be compelling, your presentation must survive comparison to a checklist of mandated ingredients. The degree to which the application garners positive checks, will determine how many points are awarded. Although those points might be many and well-earned, the only thing that matters in terms of winning the grant is if you attain more of them than your competitors. In the case of the largest and most desired grant opportunities, expect the number of competitors to be daunting.

The challenge of preparing proposals for these opportunities is elevated by the character, word and/or page limitations that are imposed for responses, even when the questions themselves all but exceed these limitations. Oh, and by the way, the application is often due within about three to four weeks of the grant announcement. Despite the challenges of these applications, I am going to assume by the fact that you are reading this book, that you have passion and enthusiasm, that you possess a great work ethic, that you care, and therefore, that you can and will succeed in winning grants. Do not be intimidated by the process. Be brave, be innovative and do not be afraid to fail. Just by trying, you are doing your job and doing it well, provided that pursuit of the grant does cause other responsibilities to fall by the wayside. I applied for and failed to win certain grants, but through that process I learned positive lessons and honed the skills that eventually resulted in victory.

While the grant writer or writing team must always specifically respond to the explicit instructions of the funder, mindful of the challenges stated above and those that are common to most grant opportunities, the following guidelines helped me to navigate the waters of grant writing successfully:

- Understand the mission, vision and core values of the grant making organization;
- Review prior projects that the organization funded;
- Prepare a clear and concise elevator speech to describe the project you are proposing;
- Create a name for the project that you are proposing that communicates that it fulfills the objective of the solicitation in an acceptable, innovative, yet proven manner, preferably conforming to a meaningful acronym;
- Create a working budget that will guide the narrative;
- Develop a one-or two-page abstract that captures all of the salient points of the narrative that includes your web site and/or any other appropriate social media links;

- Provide a narrative that includes the following elements, notwithstanding other instructions provided by the grant maker, generally in the order listed:
  - Briefly summarize your project plan;
  - Indicate the amount of funding you are requesting;
  - Provide an environmental scan of the regional and/or local economy, industry sectors, labor market, relevant geography, population demographics, and education system; (In my experience, excellent sources for this information have been available through some of our state partners, such as the New York State Department of Labor, which publishes a variety of helpful resources, such as the following: "Employment in New York State,"[132] "Labor Market Briefing,"[133] "Significant Industries;"[134] and the Empire State Development's Long Island Regional Economic Development Council, which publishes an annual progress report;[135]
  - Define the problem you plan to solve (cite compelling and well-sourced data, moving citations, evidence-based practices, as appropriate);
  - Describe your organization, including its relevant its experience, accomplishments, financial capability;
  - Describe the scope of work you will perform in detail, including your innovative application of evidence-based practices;
  - Describe the organizational partnerships and qualify the resources (in-kind and or financial) that you will leverage to perform the work;
  - Describe how the project will be managed, including leadership, strategy, planning, recording-keeping, finance/accounting, data collection and reporting;
  - Describe the <u>functions</u> of a leadership team, i.e., board of directors, steering committee, CEO, supervisory personnel, staff, volunteers, etc.

---

[132] https://content.govdelivery.com/accounts/nysdol/bulletins/35c2a5e
[133] https://dol.gov/labor-market-briefings
[134] https://dol.gov/labor/significant-industries-2021
[135] https://regionalcouncils.ny.gov/file/liredc-annual-report-2022

- ➤ Describe the qualifications of the leadership team, i.e., board of directors, CEO, supervisory personnel, staff, volunteers, etc.
- ➤ Provide an organization chart as an attachment;
- ➤ Provide a work flow chart as an attachment;
- ➤ Provide a logic model as an attachment;
- ➤ Cite the goals of the project and provide the metrics by which success will be measured, building in processes for continuous improvement, including customer feedback, if appropriate, and fact-based management techniques;
- ➤ Describe the process you will implement to collect and disseminate best practices;
- ➤ Provide a detailed sustainability plan that will describe how the project will continue to operate after the funding period ends, including the maintenance of the project's governance structure, partnerships, resources, activities, database, etc.
- Attach unique letters of commitment and support, not form letters;
- Provide a budget which includes the following elements, generally in the order listed, with a clear description of which portions will be grant funded, and which will be supported by other funds:
  - ➤ List the Staff Salaries, including full-time equivalents (FTEs) that benefit the project;
  - ➤ List the Fringe Benefits, corresponding to the full-time equivalent (FTEs) that benefit the project;
  - ➤ List the Equipment, Supplies, Marketing Expenses, Other Overhead, and the Indirect Cost Rate, if applicable
  - ➤ A budget narrative that describes each cost item in detail and how these items specifically correlate to the project narrative.
  - ➤ An itemized description of in-kind contributions that your organization will offer to the project.

Grant writing is risky business. Sometimes, to your pleasant surprise, you might actually win a grant, only to be greeted by complaints from your organization of "who is going to do this? How can we operate this?" When a workforce system is already functioning on core funding, the cynical view could be "why do we need this?" Then there are performance accountability and fiscal requirements to consider. The answer to these negative concerns is to utilize a collaborative group that includes, but is not necessarily limited to the system power structure, to properly evaluate the conceived grant project to obtain approval and consensus before applying.

Despite all of these precautions, the conundrum might still arise in which the good news is that you have won the grant, and the bad news is that you have won the grant. But fear not, as a living organism, a workforce development system cannot survive in a state of inertia. It must evolve, change and grow, lest it die. In my career, I have aspired to serve, not only as a grant writer, but in a larger sense, as a planner, and in an even larger sense, as a leader. Developing a grant project, from conception to inception is the work of a planner who is a leader, whose job is to plan the work and to work the plan. I encourage you to be courageous for the sake of innovation, sustainability and growth, all the while considering that it might be up to the operations staff to deliver on the promises you make in your application. Can it bring more, or different work? Yes, but with passion and enthusiasm that work will be accomplished successfully and it will bring a return-on-investment to the workers and the many constituencies they serve.

Finally, a workforce development professional should approach grant writing and grant execution with integrity and sincerity. That means that you refrain from making promises that you do not intend to keep in the application solely to win the grant. Should your application be innovative and therefore break new ground for your organization? Yes, but be sure that your organization can stand and balance itself on that ground. Integrity and sincerity in the world of workforce development grants mean that you intend to do what you say you will do. And that means that even if you are awarded the grants and subsequently run into an obstacle, or many obstacles that prevent your organization from following through, it is incumbent upon you and your team to find solutions. Often it is possible to work with the funding source to modify the original project as proposed. In fact, I believe that many funders embrace this type of in-process amendment because the grant was meant to discover new approaches to solving old problems.

Many funders require progress reports. You should take the reporting process seriously and therefore prepare your periodic reports with the same passion and enthusiasm that you applied to your original proposal. While it is true that without receiving the grant your project might not exist, ask yourself what is the point of operating the project, particularly with taxpayer or foundation money, if the project does not achieve at least a portion of its promised outcomes? If those outcomes are not being achieved, the workforce development professional must diligently attempt to ascertain why this is so, and then, lead the process of making the adjustments to get the project back on track. Nothing is more dangerous for our system than to take the money and run, and then, whether intentional or not, to fail to deliver on the grant project. Think of your workforce development grant project as a new park, a miracle drug, or a potential championship sports team. Then think about the difference of what happens if those projects either never fulfill their plans or potential, or if they temporarily seem to touch the stratosphere of success, only to sink, then crash and burn. In most cases, it would be better if the project never existed, and therefore, also that the grant application was never developed. Indeed, those are sad and absurd consequences, but they can be real. Publicly funded failures often become news. What could have been a landmark, can become an eyesore, what could have been a panacea, can become a pariah, and what could have been a champion, can become a loser. If unfulfilled promises in the workforce development industry enter the public consciousness, the decades of work applied by the workforce community could be undermined and potentially fatally injured. Therefore, as a workforce development professional, I appeal to you to take another road, aspire to build something that not only lasts, but prospers. As mentioned above, grant projects require sustainability plans. Those plans must be sincerely created, cultivated and implemented.

In addition to applying for grants, a workforce development professional can possibly expand the footprint of their organization and enhance its image by applying for and attaining industry-based awards. In fact, as you imagine, design and create projects and programs, I recommend that you do so with the intention of creating a winner in terms of innovation and impact. Similar to the grant development process in several ways, you must choose award applications that are relevant to the work of your organization, you must tell a compelling story that includes what need the project fulfills, and you must quantify success, both financially and in terms of performance outcomes. I encourage you to apply for grants and award opportunities, you never know, you just might win.

Chapter XV
If This is an Emergency...

Have you called the office of a health care provider recently? If you have, it is likely before you could listen to the telephone prompt containing the numerical entry you needed to make an appointment, or to conduct any other business, a recorded voice told you something like, "if this is an emergency, hang up and dial 911." Upon reflection, it seems that it is important to provide this information right up front, especially considering that while experiencing an emergency situation a human being might not think to hang up first, or to even call 911. On the other hand, after encountering these same instructions on so many occasions, it might give the caller pause to think "are there that many people out there that do not realize that they have an emergency?" Apparently, there are. And since aspiring workforce development professionals are people too, we might, not only not perceive the existence of an emergency, but also what our role in the emergency situation might or might not be.

Included in the most profound emergencies to impact our profession were the tragic events of September 11, 2001. The mere mention of that date can release a flood of memories of a day of terror, along with the fear, sadness, grief and devastation that followed for many days. That emergency presented many challenges to the world, to our nation and to our industry. It disrupted national, state, local and "family" economies. In some cases, breadwinners were killed. In others, job losses ultimately occurred due to indirect ripple effects in our economy. This situation was another example of where a challenge to workforce development professionals became an opportunity. It became an opportunity for us to do our part to help our nation and its workforce to recover. Those in the workforce community who successfully rose to meet this challenge recognized at an early stage that it would be necessary to disseminate program application information to individuals who, in some cases felt lost and confused, who had not accessed our services in the past, to amend welcoming processes to accommodate those who were in shock, to create new career pathways, or to re-imagine existing career pathways for dislocated workers, all the while pursuing new sources of funding appropriate to these tasks.

Another example of an emergency that impacts upon workforce development is when natural disasters occur, such as earthquakes, floods, wild fires, tornadoes and hurricanes. In these instances, workforce development professionals must rise to the occasion again. There are also more subtle emergencies that might challenge us, as well. The Financial Crisis of 2007 and 2008, also known as the Global Financial Crisis, wreaked havoc on the economy of the New York Metropolitan Area. In response to that crisis, among other actions taken, the board I worked for successfully applied for and was awarded a U.S. Department of Labor Regional Innovation Grant, which not only assisted our region to envision, plan and implement a strategy to deal with the crisis, but also to improve our systems to better deal with future emergencies. Fortunately, the boards in our region were functioning at appropriate levels of efficiency to both win and implement the grant.

The ability of a workforce development system to create and to implement a plan to respond to dire and unforeseen circumstances is largely dependent upon the degree to which it has established and maintained sound management practices in less challenging times. In this sense, the ability of our systems to respond to emergencies is largely determined by how diligently we perform our functions on a daily basis, as described in the preceding chapters entitled: "The System," "The System, Center, Program Paradox," and "Beyond Business Services..." For example, the chapter entitled "Beyond Business Services...," includes the following relevant passage related to the workforce development board function of "Brokering:" "A basic tenet of emergency management is that in an emergency a traditional chain of command may be temporarily suspended to establish a functional management structure that is the most responsive to the problem at hand. Under this type of scenario, egos are truly checked at the door and the team members focus on mission above status, credit, and other distractions. A similar phenomenon takes shape when workforce development professionals engage in brokering. Once we establish a regular schedule for convening business services leaders, we can leverage the resources of this captive audience to create outstanding and imaginative workforce development programs."

Imagine how much more efficiently a local board will respond to an emergency that is not only unforeseen, but perhaps unimagined, if it has a sound brokering system in place. In this sense, the workforce development professional must take all of the statutorily required functions of the board seriously and do their part to ensure that the board not only complies with the statute, but also, that the workforce development system becomes part of an infrastructure that can withstand the worst emergency, empowering the board to fulfill its role in helping the people it serves to recover and prosper in their post-emergency lives.

A final example of how an emergency or disaster was recognized as a challenge and then transformed into an opportunity to improve services was the Coronavirus Pandemic, or COVID-19. Again, responding to an unforeseen and almost unimaginable crisis, workforce development professionals across the Nation moved with rapid agility to enhance their information technology capacities and to revise their procedures, either to expand or to create remote operating systems, so that job seekers and businesses could still be served while career centers were closed due to quarantines. Those professionals who adapted to a new environment in the face of these extraordinary challenges and who, as a result, created new opportunities for better services, were most likely those who were in a posture of continuous improvement and dedication to excellence as a standard operating procedure before there ever was an emergency. Clearly, this posture was developed through a dedication born of passion and enthusiasm for their work, leaving imagination at their fingertips. The best time to read about and understand the WIOA requirements for emergency and disaster assistance is before a crisis occurs. This information is included in the WIOA law at Section *170 - NATIONAL DISLOCATED WORKER GRANTS.*

Chapter XVI
Fiscal

In the chapter on "Performance Leadership," we discouraged a leadership style signified by a leader who proudly proclaims ignorance of the intricacies of Performance Indicators, while assuring skeptics that mastery of the subject is delegated to a subordinate. The same advice pertains to fiscal management, which should not be ignored or marginalized. With the disclaimer that the author is not an attorney, an accountant, or a spokesman for any agency or organization, below are suggested functions and levels of involvement that I believe might assist workforce development leaders seeking to ensure proper fiscal management:

Budgeting

WIOA requires that the local board approve a budget on an annual basis in accordance the following passage:
"...The local board shall develop a budget for the activities of the local board in the local area, consistent with the local plan and the duties of the local board under this section, subject to the approval of the chief elected official."[136]

While modern banking seems to render the question "can you balance a checkbook?" as somewhat archaic, we do not have to imagine a small booklet of tear away checks, a log of checks written and tear away deposits slips in order to envision our individual responsibility to manage our personal finances. This responsibility remains, whether we are checking balances on our smart phone, or doing things the old-fashioned way. This same responsibility must be accepted by workforce leaders. While this responsibility might seem academic to many, the type of leader who delegates this responsibility to others, whom they believe possess an arcane fiscal

---

[136] Public Law 113-128, Section 107 (d)(12)(A)

expertise, is unwittingly and unnecessarily entering the precarious position of one day being informed, or coming to the shocking conclusion on their own, that funds are being mismanaged.

Mismanagement might be manifest in over expenditures, under expenditures, improper cost allocation, improper reporting, improper accounting, or worse. The "worse" in this context might be questioned or disallowed costs, fraud, bribery, embezzlement...you get the idea. Proper fiscal practices begin with proper management practices in general, which lead to proper budgeting practices. The development and management of a budget is ultimately a chief executive officer function, not that of a fiscal manager, accountant or other delegate. This is because the operational or program planning that begins in the board room with a creative vision and evolves to a world class system must be conceived with, and tethered to, a well-designed budget. Efficient co-dependency of program planning and budgetary management and development are often a determinant of the success or failure of workforce development system, as well as the foundation for true workforce development professionalism.

In my view, local board staff should continuously monitor system and program planning and performance in tandem with the budget planned versus actual expenditures. These staff should report regularly to the board's executive committee, and also at appropriate intervals to the full board membership. I suggest that a new budget should be approved at a full membership board meeting at least once per year and that major budget modifications should be reviewed by the board on a timely basis. Positive or negative budgetary outcomes do not exist in a financial vacuum independent of system and program planned versus actual goals and outcomes. For example, under expenditure usually equates to under enrollment in training programs, which through regressive analysis should guide leaders to examine their operations related to recruitment, assessment, training program enrollment, quality of service providers, alignment of program openings with labor market information and beyond. The fiscal numbers are "sexy" because they are indicators of the quality of the entire workforce development system. This is because the numbers, both, fiscal and performance, planned versus actual, are the windows through which that leader must peer into the central nervous system of the workforce development system.

Evaluation of the productive interplay of program planning and budgetary planning and performance are so essential to good workforce development management that I believe workforce leaders should develop and regularly utilize a reporting system that measures both disciplines and generates reporting data that can be reduced to what I referred to earlier as a "single page." That page should be reviewed by leadership and appropriate staff on a regular basis, with its tributaries of supporting data discussed and reviewed as appropriate.

Cost Allocation Plan

Imagine, if you will, the image of a person casting cash into open boxes labeled with signs that designate a host of allowable WIOA costs, such as the following: "Equipment," "Staff," "Office Space," "Printing," "Consultants," "Overhead," etc. These are just a few examples of expenditures which are necessary for system and program operations, and for which a determination of how they should be allocated cannot be made without more information. The information needed is the use of these items. In other words, what funding stream will they benefit? Will it be WIOA Adult, Youth or Dislocated Worker? Or, will the funds benefit a special grant, either under WIOA or another source? Furthermore, within the funding stream, will the expenditure serve a function that is properly categorized under the Administration cost category or the Program cost category? Or, to complicate things further, will the expenditure benefit multiple funding streams and or cost categories, i.e., Administration and/or Program? The answers to these questions will tell us if the cost of the expenditure is to be treated as "direct," "shared direct" or "indirect." If the cost is to be treated under any of the latter categories, then it is necessary to have in place uniform and consistently applied allocation methods. These methods must be documented in a cost allocation plan that conforms to the Code of Federal Regulations and is approved by the full membership of the board at least once per year. I recommend developing a cost allocation worksheet for all procured items in the form of a matrix that designates all of the above funding streams and cost categories, with fields for checking off which of those designations apply. A hard copy of the form should be maintained for an auditor's review in each vendor or subrecipient file. A similar worksheet should be developed and maintained to demonstrate methods of procurement, i.e., small purchase, request for proposals (RFP), bid, sole source, federal or state contract.

A true professional is confident in their ability to gain a command of the statutory and regulatory requirements for documentation and administrative functions, including cost allocation and procurement. Professionals want to show their work and demonstrate their thought processes, as well as their dedication to diligence. Workforce development professionals should consider grant oversight authorities and auditors to be colleagues who share their zeal to for constant integrity and continually improving levels of efficiency. Those pursuits can only be attained through transparency and the existence of processes to identify and correct errors. We cannot expect to be perfect, but we should still always strive for perfection, both in the character and the operation of our programs.

Monitoring Minimum and Maximum Expenditure Requirements

WIOA imposes several requirements for minimum and maximum levels of expenditures. These levels are underlined below.

- Local areas must spend a minimum of 80% of an allotment in the first year that the funds are allotted under the WIOA Adult, Youth and Dislocated Worker funding streams with each funding stream evaluated separately.

The law states:

"The amount available for re-allotment for a program year for programs funded under subsection (b)(1)(B) (relating to adult employment and training) or for programs funded under subsection (b)(2)(B) (relating to dislocated worker employment and training) is equal to the amount by which the unobligated balance of the State allotments for adult employment and training activities or dislocated worker employment and training activities, respectively, at the end of the program year prior to the program year for which the

determination under this paragraph is made, exceeds 20 percent of such allotments for the prior program year."[137]

- <u>75% of funds allocated under the WIOA Youth funding stream must be spent on programs for out-of-school youth.</u>

The law states:
"For any program year, not less than 75 percent of the funds allotted under section 127(b)(1)(C), reserved under section 128(a), and available for statewide activities under subsection (b), and not less than 75 percent of funds available to local areas under subsection (c), shall be used to provide youth workforce investment activities for out-of-school youth".[138]

- <u>A maximum of 10 percent a local area's WIOA allocation may be spent for costs allocated to the category of Administration.</u>

The law states:
"Of the amount allocated to a local area under this subsection and section 133(b) for a fiscal year, not more than 10 percent of the amount may be used by the local board involved for the administrative costs of carrying out local workforce investment activities under this chapter or chapter 3."[139]

In order to determine what costs should be allocated to the Administration cost category, it is important to understand what the law defines as administrative costs. The WIOA Final Rule defines these costs in under Section 683.215.

Miscellaneous Other Functions

In addition to the functions and levels of involvement discussed above, workforce development professionals in a leadership role should oversee, to an appropriate level, the following fiscal functions:

---

[137] Public Law 113-128, Section 132 (c)(2)
[138] Public Law 113-128, Section 129 (a)(4)(A)
[139] Public Law 113-128, Section 128 (b)(4)(A)

- Cash Management
- Reporting;
- Procurement;
- Payroll;
- Personnel Time and Attendance Tracking;
- Inventory;
- Sub-recipient Monitoring;
- Property Management;
- Audit Resolution;
- Development and reconciliation of a Resource Sharing Agreement in accordance with the local memorandum of understanding (MOU).

Chapter XVII
Having "The Talk" with Kids

Most parents can speak with their children about almost any topic, but there is one topic that many find difficult to discuss. Perhaps they feel constricted by societal traditions. Perhaps they do not feel that they have appropriate science-based understanding of the topic. In any event, at an age that they deem appropriate, and as radical as it might seem, as early as possible, parents should have "the talk" with their kids. Of course, the topic of the talk I am referring to is "workforce development." Seriously, it is a difficult subject, particularly in consideration of the fact that everything around us is changing so rapidly and that the speed of change will exponentially accelerate as our children age. For this reason, rather than simply advising our kids about workforce development, I believe that parents and children should conduct research, learn about and understand this topic together.

Included in the "everything" changing so rapidly includes the elements of technology, the culture, the products, the human resources infrastructure and the language of the workplace. The elements are often combined, sometimes unpredictably with local, state, national and world events that might range from war, to pandemic, to famine, to natural disasters, to scientific discoveries, inventions, financial changes, popular culture, sports phenomena etc. Parents and their supporters in education, faith-based organizations, economic development, government, business, community-based, commerce and fraternal organization, and more, all need to understand the positive impact that they can have in developing the workforce of tomorrow. I believe that our society needs to apply its resources to help our children to be properly oriented to the workplace that they will spend much of their life working in one day, not only for the benefit of the children, but for the future of our society and our quality of life.

Acknowledgements

In Chapter 2, I wrote "...even during the briefest exchange...a life can be significantly changed for the better in an instant." I know this to be true because of the countless people to whom I owe an enormous debt of gratitude for helping me. While I appreciate those who enhanced my life, sometimes dramatically during brief interactions, the limitless appreciation I feel increases with time for those who have accompanied me over the longest periods. With the exception of the NYATEP officers that I mentioned, I have decided not to acknowledge others by name, but I believe that they will take pride in knowing that I am referring to them when I humbly offer the following notes of appreciation.

    I wish to thank my family for their love and support; the local elected officials, workforce development board officers and members, commissioners, deputy commissioners, and staff that provided me with sound leadership, challenges to be innovative, opportunities for growth, and generous esprit de corps; the partner organizations, consultants and contractors with whom I enjoyed teamwork and assistance; the businesses and job seekers who provide trust, cooperation and participation in the workforce development system; the federal and state-level leaders and staff with whom I worked, of whom I often said always have their hearts and their heads in the right place, and who guided me on my professional journey; the leaders, staff, board and membership of NYATEP and other workforce development associations and organizations, including non-profits, community-based organizations, organized labor, health care, charitable and humanitarian organizations, who help bring out the best in all of us. Thank you to the many friends and co-workers by whose friendship I have been truly blessed, and especially those who were there for me during the toughest of times. Thank you to all who shared their insight, wit and wisdom to inspire me to be a better person, to continue to aspire to be a workforce development professional and to write this book. Last but not least, I wish to thank you, the reader, for allowing me to share a few ideas that might just improve our industry and help you to help more people along the way.

Final Note

My deepest thanks to my editor, Em Hughes, an extremely accomplished individual who lent her talents to this book, and also, to my proofreader, who helped immeasurably, but choose to remain anonymous.

Bibliography

https://www.nyatep.org

https://www.nist.gov

https:/dol.gov./agencies/odep/program-areas/customized-employment

Workforce Innovation Opportunity Act of 2014
www.dol.gov/agencies/eta/wioa/

Training and Employment Information Notice No. 12-98, United States Department of Labor, October 8, 1998

https://www.federalregister-gov/documents/2000/08/11/00-19985/workforce-investment-act

https://www.govinfo.gov/content/pkg/STATUTE-107/pdf/STATUTE-107- Pg285.pdf

Customized Employment - United States Department of Labor
www.dol.gov/agencies/odep/program-areas/customized-employment

Government Performance and Results Act of 1993
https://www.govinfo.gov/content/pkg/STATUTE-107/pdf/STATUTE-107-Pg285.pdf

Training and Employment Guidance Letter Number 19-16 Operating Guidance for Workforce Innovation and Opportunity Act, Employment and Training Advisory System, United States Department of Labor, March 1, 2017
www.dol.gov/agencies/eta/advisories/training-and-employment-guidance-letter-no-19-16

Federal Register: Workforce Innovation and Opportunity Act Effectiveness in Serving Employers Performance Indicator

https:/www.careeronestop.org/competencymodel

https://www.careeronestop.org/competencymodel/getstarted/eta-industry-competency-initiative.aspx

Training and Employment Guidance Letter Number 21-16 Operating Guidance for Workforce Innovation and Opportunity Act, Employment and Training Advisory System, United States Department of Labor, March 2, 2017
www.dol.gov/agencies/eta/advisories/training-and-employment-guidance-letter-no-21-16

https://www.dol.gov/agencies/eta/performance/reporting

https://content.govdelivery.com/accounts/nysdol/bulletins/35c2a5e

https://dol.gov/labor-market-briefings

https://dol.gov/labor/significant-industries-2021

https://regionalcouncils.ny.gov/file/liredc-annual-report-2022

20 Code of Federal Regulations 683.215
https//www.ecfr.gov/current/title-20/chapter-V/part-683/subpart-B/section-683.215

About the Author

Edward Kenny has worked in the workforce development industry for over 43 years. He served in a variety of managerial positions, and primarily, as the planner for the Town of Hempstead/City Local Workforce Development Board. In that capacity, he designed several state and national award-winning programs. The Board presented Ed with its *Leadership Award* and the United Way of Long Island presented him with its *Workforce Hero Award*. Ed has served as a Board Member of the New York Association of Training and Employment Professionals (NYATEP), as the Vice Chair of the Nassau Community College Local Advisory Council, as the President of the Nassau BOCES Citizens Advisory Council, and as Chair of the New York State Dislocated Worker Task Force. He has a Bachelor's Degree in Business Management from Adelphi University and was designated as a certified trainer of the U. S. Department of Labor. Ed has presented at numerous workforce development conferences throughout the Nation. His volunteer service includes coaching for the Connetquot Soccer League, Lindenhurst Soccer League, Lindenhurst American Little League, Loyal Order of the Moose, the Knights of Columbus and Island Harvest. Ed also served as a Vice President and Track Program Coordinator for the Our Lady of Perpetual Help CYO, where he also coached track and basketball. He is a recipient of the *Nassau-Suffolk CYO Role Model Award*. At Old Bethpage Restoration Village, he served as a volunteer Old Time Baseball player. Also, a playwright and lyricist, Ed has published several verse plays, musical librettos and books of lyrics and poetry through his publishing company, Bluebird Publishing. He is a member of The Dramatists Guild of America and ASCAP. For More Information Contact: edwardjjkenny@gmail.com.

www.ingramcontent.com/pod-product-compliance
Lightning Source LLC
Chambersburg PA
CBHW032144100725
29452CB00011B/55